The New

Preface

The revelations and wisdom in this book

Are designed to make you think

And, perhaps get involved.

Please read this book!

I urge you to read it!

I dare you to read it!

I beg you to read it!

If you do,

I guarantee you will

READ IT AGAIN

And AGAIN!!!

DISCLAIMER

This book was written and copyrighted in the year 2000. Keep in mind that much of the information is dated, but still true. Please be aware that I am currently working on a follow-up book that will detail and quantify the issues discussed here. In addition, I will update you on the progress of the task given to me by My Maker.

I truly hope that this book wets your appetite for knowledge and motivates you to get involved.

Humbly
Willie R. Harvey

Special Acknowledgement

I am eternally grateful to Mitchelle Honore", who edited and formatted this work for me. I appreciate her formidable skills, enthusiasm and willingness to assist in her many areas of expertise. I personally, and this significant project is highly blessed by her involvement.

TABLE OF CONTENTS

TABLE OF CONTENTS (Continued)

TABLE OF CONTENTS (Continued)

GREETING

To all of you, I greet you in the name of mankind.

You may want to know who I am and why I feel qualified to come before you, greeting you in the name of mankind. I have prepared a biographical sketch to save time. I will just touch on some things that, hopefully you will find of interest.

My life has not always been good. I've had my ups and downs. One day, a short time ago, I like to refer to it as a short period of time, I was thinking how blessed I am. Thinking, to me is tantamount to communing with the Creator. I thought, "Lord, You are so wonderful and I am so blessed. Just reveal to me what you would have me to do so I can go do it. Let my life be a testament to You."

INTRODUCTION

I realize that through my travels and hopefully thousands of speaking engagements, I will encounter people who hold different religious views from mine. I sincerely hope and pray that what I say and who I am does not offend or cause anyone to close their mind to this message.

Soon after my surrender to the will of the Creator, thoughts began to formulate in my mind. So many pieces of a puzzle that I would wake up, get up, and start writing. I realized that if I waited until later, it would be too late. To wait would be to forget.

I pondered: What does this all mean? All of these short thoughts. Will I someday publish them, maybe write a book? It became an obsession. I couldn't get my mind free of the pieces.

I remembered the praise and the request that I made. And suddenly it came to me! You asked, now receive. Be patient and let Him do His thing. And He did over the next five months. This is His thing, manifested through me, his humble servant.

1

He answered all of my questions and concerns. He showed me that this was in His plans long before I was ready. It took a while, but, He allowed me to soar, then brought me low and caused me to reflect back on a thought He gave me 30 years ago:

"Let's go OUT-WAY OUT,
Where Nature is herself,
Where man is MAN and a tree is a TREE,
Where waters run endlessly,
Where there is no need
For a spoken language, But all commune
And understand.
Where mountains, forest, lakes and sand
Loom greater than the greatest MAN.
Let us humble ourselves to the Greatness around,
And contemplate from whence we came."

One day, when the time was right, when I was ready, He revealed Alpha and Omega, then all the pieces fell into place.

I hope you can come with me on this mission, review these thoughts and let yourself imagine the possibilities, and then ACT!!

My life's mission is to share an inspired look at man's humble beginning, and to point out some milestones and signposts. I see where man has developed and where he went astray. My mind has been given special insight to divine plans for mankind. I have been shown a way for man to finally reach the goal set for him from the beginning.

A PRAYER

Lord, as I wonder through many strange lands,

 Let me remain Thy servant.

Lord, as I associate with those of

 Diverse theologies,

  Let me remember Thy teachings.

Lord, as I walk among those of

 Different lands,

  Guide my feet in the path of Thy glory.

CHAPTER ONE: THEORY

NEW PHILOSOPHY

Today, I would like to introduce a New Philosophy. I will point out some of the signposts and share with you some of the things that prepared me to finally accept what has been put on my heart to share with the world.

It's been centuries since someone devoted time to man's reason for being: How man should relate to each other and what we can expect will become of us all. When I finish, I hope you will be stimulated to look into it and come to some conclusions of your own.

Consider, for a moment, the implications of all the people on earth working toward the same goals. Having the same morals and in harmony with the big picture.

Imagine a world where wars are not needed. A world free from hunger; where everyone has at least the necessities, a world, where everyone has a sense of purpose and a feeling of belonging.

Consider the Christian Philosophy

GOD created man in HIS own image. Shaped from the elements, GOD breathed the breath of life in man and gave him a SOUL. To keep man from being lonesome, he gave him woman as a mate. He and his mate were placed in the garden and surrounded with all they needed. Along came the DEVIL in the form of the serpent and corrupted God's creation. Man sinned. Not the first time, but MAN SINNED. God's displeasure is evident as he expelled man from the garden and removed THE TREE OF LIFE. Man was condemned to toil and woman punished to bare children, to have children, not grown men and women.

Man started out as one man (Adam) who was destined to please God. He sinned and has been trying to get back to that point every since. Everything that man does is pre-ordained. He has to pay the price by accomplishing a special task. Man has to mature and return to his original state. Back to the one who can commune with God.

THINKERS

There was a time when men of great statue would sit around and THINK. They would contemplate from whence we came. A poem that I wrote 30 years ago expresses this:

Contemplation

They tried to make sense of the birth and life of man.

They tried to give purpose to man's existence.

These men became the pillars of our society.

They theorized and formulated our reasons for being.

They explained how the universe was created.

Since then, only a few men and women have dared to look at new possibilities. They dare to continue to be the real thinkers and philosophers. One exciting glimpse has been Gandhi with his philosophy on passivism[1]. Dr. Martin L. King refined it to non-violent resistance.

For hundreds of years, man has been content to accept the handful of major philosophies. We have concentrated on ways to exist within each of them, at the same time allowing the others to exist also. We try to live and let live. As long as there are two or more of these, there will always be a revelry or competiveness in ways to live, why we exist and the overall purpose of things. Could I be the next in a long line of philosophers? In time this question will find its own answer.

There have been events in my life that, at the time, meant little more than humor to me. Now recalling as many as possible, I can see direction growing out of many years of molding.

---

[1] See Gahandi on Page 93.

The New Revelation – Putting It All Together

I recently had a revelation. Something came over me, and thoughts formulated that I couldn't forget. I realized that when I have those ideas I should quickly write them down or I will not remember them. As I make these notes, I look back on the many times I have had these experiences and said I would remember them. But an hour later they would be fond memories of thought patterns that I couldn't remember.

I remember my experience of being struck by lightning or rather lightning striking all around me and not striking me. I remember the advice the doctor gave me when I developed ulcers in high school: "Leave home and learn to laugh out loud". I remember playing poker with the boys on Fridays and realizing that I made as much money as all of them put together. I remember not paying taxes and how that affected everything I tried to do. It kept me from pursuing my real aspirations (those skeletons in the closets!) I remember living on the edge and letting everyone think otherwise. I remember being at a party in Los Angeles. During the conversation, we were discussing the state of affairs. As I was talking, a man in the gathering just burst out "I believe you. I like that. Just tell me what to do and I'm with you". I remember how scared I got at the thought of that "find of power." I remember shopping at the Everett Mall and stopping to rest. A lady sat down and we began to pass the time. We talked about kids, choices, education etc. She asked if I would be willing to come to her child's school and speak at an assembly. I remember working in Nagoya and feeling all alone. But I was treated like visiting royalty when my wife and I went sightseeing and traveling in Japan. I remember being used by a friend. I remember my feelings of family and how much they failed me. I remember when I first gave serious thought to death and came to grips with my eventual end. When I really considered my religion and began to go to Bible study.

I realize that knowing God's purpose in marriage could have saved me lots of pain and sorrow. This knowledge could have kept me married to the first Mrs. Harvey. The more I leveled with myself, the more clearly I could see how arrogant I was toward others. To realize the truth doesn't keep one from suffering the consequences. My life took a drastic turn for the worst.

I remember being unemployed for two years and realizing how little money it took to live a good life. My thoughts sustained me. Being down didn't worry me; I understood what I was going through but surely wished it would soon be over.

The most humbling experiences were going to Los Angeles to be with my father as he went through radiation therapy for six months.

I have had lots of time to think. The thoughts just won't go away. After discussing it with some close friends, I concluded that I must pursue this course of action. I believe God really speaks to me. To hear him clearly, I must be quiet enough to hear, and then obey. As I pursue this philosophy, I realize that not my will, but Thy will, oh Lord, be done.

A good friend offered this advice: "I truly feel this is a calling of which you seem to be afraid. You need to fast and pray. The answers you seek will be revealed to you. I feel this is what the Lord has put me here to say to you." Thank you, Evone[2].

Thoughts of man's existence and our reasons for existence have haunted me as long as I can remember. At the age of twenty, I wrote down my thoughts (Let's go out, way out, etc. See poems). Since then, I have had only a few such thoughts. I regret not taking time to write all of them down. My beliefs about family caused me to write, "Be a Parent".

It has been said, "If you call a deceased person's name, you keep the person alive for ever." To all the people of the past I look forward to seeing you and learning your names. Until then I dedicate "Heaven" to you.

I believe in God and take my direction from Him, because I know what's behind door number two.

Man truly is the product of God's mind, a product that's still under construction.

---

[2] Evone Riley.

God made man and blew the breath of Life in him. He created man with a Soul. Man will be born and die in the flesh but the Soul will live forever. The one thing man will never be able to do is create a Soul. Beyond that, well, the product is still under construction.

To those of you who express a fear of technology; who are afraid of computers – I say that's good. No matter how simple we like to think it is to operate computers, they can be challenging, even to those who know them well.

Today my computer crashed due to a computer virus. Now I can't get Windows 98 to boot up. I've been working in the "Safe Mode" but can't figure out what is wrong. Even I need help sometimes. I'm really happy to have a friend in Pat Henry who built my computer and promises to give me all the help I need learning to use the software.

Never forget your friends.
Always remember to say thank you.

HAVE'S AND HAVE-NOT'S, "GREED"

As far back as man can remember there has always been the common thread that runs true through the entire world, those who have and those who want or need. There are people who can do things, produce products, and say things (poets, ministers, philosophers).

What they do fills a void in us, fills a need, or makes us feel good. The link between them and all the rest of us is they have something we want. And, they are more than willing to share it. They offer it for sale.

Everything from the beginning that has happened can be grouped into categories. Periods of time, spans of time, in which certain thought patterns or philosophies molded everything. The first thing that falls into this pattern is man and woman. The oldest profession is said to be prostitution. This sets the mold for everything else that has ever happened. Out of this came all the morals and living standards that have ever challenged man. Out of this came all the religions. Countries and nations were formed because of the needs that came from sexual relations. According to how you believe the need for male/female relations preceded the need for food or shelter – they were provided by the divine creator. Once man and woman realized that what one has the other wants, he can sell and acquire that which is precious to both of them.

The more people who are born, the more needs will come about. Two people could huddle under a tree. Ten people would need a cave. One hundred people would need to be mobile so they could gather enough food. Their dwellings would have to be mobile or found as they traveled. Bands of nomads moved from place to place in search of food. As they encountered other groups they discovered other ways of acquiring food and shelter besides force. They traded product and services. They shared their folklore and entertainment.

The need for survival by now had gone through many minute changes and metamorphosis. The system of exchanging needed goods and services became quite sophisticated. People wanted equal portions for a determined exchange. Measures were agreed upon. The things that were exchanged often were cumbersome and hard to move. Money in all of its forms became a common item of exchange. Because of money, anyone could exchange what he or she had that others needed. Then, take the money and acquire what they wanted from anyone within traveling distance. Each kingdom produced its own form of money and determined its value.

Not only was there a need for survival and protection, but a desire (want) for pleasures and comforts soon became the driving force. Once one acquired all they needed, they did not stop acquiring and greed set in. The more you have the less you need and to acquire more is GREED.

There came a time when people settled on land and raised farm animals. They raised chickens, sheep, cattle, etc. They grew crops to support their food needs and traded with their neighbors. Now they could grow any crop or raise any animal they chose. They could trade products for money and money for products, as needed. As kingdoms/cities developed there came a need for people to do more types of work than farming. Such large numbers were needed that training had to be provided. Training became a new service. If you could train you would be paid for that skill. You could exchange your talent for training for whatever you needed or you could get paid in money, and then buy whatever you needed.

Good and, eventually, great institutions of learning were developed. The development of these learning institutes created a need for teachers to the develop methods of teaching. This created an understanding how to learn, or what to learn. People learned only what they needed in order to perform a particular task. The instructors in these institutions realized that they had to teach many different things, but everyone could not learn all things. They had to devise a way to teach everyone the basics so that as the need arose they could be taught what was needed to perform a specific job. Fields of study were developed. Science, Arts, Languages, Trades, Mathematics, and Theology were all formulated. These institutions of learning became a field of endeavor of themselves. They changed mans' outlook on himself and spawn the pure thinkers.

People that had amassed many possessions now found themselves with plenty of time to do anything they wanted, other than work. So they began to think of ways to challenge their minds. They went to schools of higher learning. Thinkers created a need and desire for pleasure. Pleasure then lead to the development of entertainment. People with great wealth would offer part of their possessions for pleasures and entertainment.

The Greed formula:

"ACQUIRE what you NEED. To acquire all you need is what you WANT. To WANT more than you need is GREED".

Greed makes people believe they need what they want. Therefore, they acquire more of what they want, which is more than they really need. MORE fueled by GREED, turns into DESIRE. Our DESIRE is to ACQUIRE. This endless circle creates a void that is filled by pleasures and entertainment. WE

10

trade wealth for services, whether it's labor, service, entertainment or pleasure. Somewhere along the way, envy and competition with our neighbor comes into existence.

People who thought they would grow up to be farmers, just like their parents, found an attraction elsewhere. Cities needed laborers and service providers. They needed people who could build, manage, plan, serve and protect. Teachers would take farmers and teach them to perform these tasks.

So farmers now learned new skills and moved to the cities where they exchanged their skills for money. The more people populated cities, the bigger the need for farmers to supply the food they required. Farmers became fewer and the needs grew bigger. Ways for fewer farmers to produce more from the land lead to the development of tools to produce the food and chemicals to help the farmers produce better crops. Someone was needed to produce these tools and chemicals. A new industry was born. The need to produce tools and machinery caused a revolution in the cities and on the farm.

Skills for many jobs were taught so the new industry could flourish. Now you could do something (perform a task which was just part of the overall job) and get paid in the common exchange – money. The Industrial Revolution was born.

Industrial Revolution

Inventions of industry became big business. Inventors could exchange their ideas for money or services as needed. Industrial minded people bought inventions and sold the products for money. They produced what people could use. They limited production to quantities that they could sell. If there was not a need or want (demand), they could not exchange (sell) the product. This gave birth to the law of supply and demand. Then that old rascal, GREED raised its head. What if you could create a demand – a want bigger than the NEED? More people would want the product causing an increase in production, therefore taking in more money. An appeal to people was developed. Today, we know it as advertising. If you tell people about a product or service, they may not know it exist and really have a need for it. Tell people about the advantages of using a product or service and create a desire for it. Advertise it in a way that appeals to their senses and create an emotion that produces a want. The WANT becomes so strong that it turns into a need. People who control the industries amass great fortunes and begin to indulge their wants with pleasure and entertainment.

We find that great fortunes and wealth are controlled by a few. The rest of us continue to work. We try to meet our basic needs for food, shelter and clothing. We become educated in a specific trade and perform a routine day after day for an agreed amount of pay. We develop special talents in medical fields, engineering and education. We learn to think and express ourselves through the Arts. These talents allow us to demand more in compensation than other jobs whose skills require only repetition. In all of them, we can trade/exchange our time and skills for money. Then we can determine what we need and have a method for obtaining it.

So the die is cast. We become the HAVEs and the HAVE-NOTs. This gives rise to the Golden Rule: "Them that's got the Gold - RULES". Money equals power. People don't rule the world. People with money and power rule the world. The rest of us just try to make it. People with money determine what we do, what we see and how we exist. They determine what jobs we should train for and how much we can earn. People with wealth determine types of entertainment and fund the Arts. They own most of the places we live, bank and work.

Through the years, things have changed very little. The formula still holds true. The things that have changed are the products and services.

In the beginning, the products and services were sex, food, shelter and clothing. We could debate the order. As time passed, greed began to control all. Man's desire for pleasure and comfort led to him constantly thinking of how to make (his) life easier and more rewarding. How to have what he wanted, not just what he needed. To protect and control his wealth, he developed cities that took

12

people from a rural farm life to city dwelling. That caused a need for tools to make people more productive. This made living in cities possible.

The need for industry created an opportunity for some to amass riches, which kept the cycle going. The better life became the bigger the need for (or want) luxuries and diversions.

The Industrial Revolution has lead to ways of producing more, faster. Training, tools to make tools, cost control and benefits all were the results. All this was designed to keep people working for them until they find methods of producing more with fewer people.

Wars around the world have contributed greatly to this process. In the beginning, there were struggles (fights) between those who had to see who could acquire the most. This competition lead to all-out wars caused by GREED. Now we know that some of the great wars really were fought over that first premise: SEX. Man wanted woman. Woman eventually realized more than one man wanted her. These men competed for the affection of a woman. If the woman had just chosen one man, we might have avoided some of those battles. Woman, seeing the effect they had, decided to exploit this competition to get what they wanted. Yes, sexual greed spawned many fights. The most powerful drive in man is sex. To please his woman and be praised by her, he will acquire all in her name.

Wars, for whatever reason, lead to the development of many products and created whole industries. The need to conquer the rival, who now is the enemy, led researchers to develop many inventions whose usefulness outlasted the wars or the supposed war-related need. The development of medicine, travel and communication all benefited from war-related research. Our space exploration was an idea for philosophers until the research showed that control of space really is an essential military requirement. I believe the development of today's computer came directly from a need to provide answers to problems in space. Mathematics showed the feasibility of space travel. The formulas needed to be refined and the percent of error reduced to an acceptable level. People were

13

asked to risk their lives and the lives of animals. These new products/industries caused a great shift in what people were taught in school. The knowledge of the world began to double every few years. Things people were trained to do twenty years before were becoming obsolete. Sometimes the occupation one studied in school, the specialty that one planned to pursue for a lifetime, was eliminated due to the invention of computers and robotics. As time marched on, the learning centers were developed to combat the lack of larger learning institutions to react quickly to these changes. A new type of teacher was required. A new method of teaching was born.

These learning centers exist to teach the requirements for new trades and jobs that never existed before. The institutions of higher learning began to realize that their methods had become obsolete; they were producing products that could not be sold. Their graduates could not find work in their learned professions. They could not exchange their talents for money. These institutions began to appeal to industry for help. What they learned revolutionized what was being taught.

Some of the people who owned and controlled these industries had attended these same institutions of higher learning. Since they graduated and were working in the real world, they had an opportunity to think and reflect back on their training. Were they really prepared for what they were doing? What did people really need to know? The answer came from the collective thoughts of many business leaders, who needed people trained to think; people who could analyze a situation and develop an approach to a solution. Since so many jobs were changing or being eliminated, the people doing those jobs most likely would need to work longer than that job would be available. They needed to be able to learn something else. The ultimate education would teach people the basics and prepares them to handle change.

Service Revolution

So, now we move from the Industrial Revolution to the Service Revolution. This concept is not new. European and Asian countries have prospered through this revolution. Most of the basic needs of people have been met with products and inventions. Greed has produced the level of pleasure and entertainment we now enjoy. The great emphasis is on providing services for our fellow man. Although products can be confined to regions, services are or will become universal. Services grew out of the wants of people, not their needs. The whole process is controlled by GREED. Greed applied correctly can be a good thing.

There're many people who can't invent products, who can't perform tasks to make the tools and products of the day. They still need to acquire the basics. These people can only appeal to the greed side of people. They can offer themselves by providing a service.

A service is a labor that requires producing no product. It requires no tools and leaves no residual effect. Once a service is rendered, it is finished. The exchange for that service is other services, goods or money.

Today we find people are reluctant to let themselves move into the service age. Traditional habits are hard to break. People are conditioned to go to school, get a good job and work until retirement. Their parents did it. Their grandparents did it and their children will do it too. Well, that might have worked but for the short sightedness of individuals when it came to preparing for retirement. People just didn't earn enough on their jobs to live well. They surely couldn't put anything aside for retirement. Those who often ran into financial catastrophes, took most of their savings from which they never recovered.

On the other hand, big businesses are trying so hard to modernize and make a profit (the almighty dollar) that they now show no loyalty to those who would like to keep a job until retirement. The need to streamline, modernize, downsize and lay off workers has created an atmosphere of distrust by the workers in all businesses. People are looking for other ways to make ends meet.

15

They realize retirement will mean (if they manage to reach it) much less income than they now have, and that is not nearly enough. Most of us do not look forward to retirement.

Others have begun to catch the fire and look for a second job. Some of us call it a part-time job because we find some kind of work that requires little education or training and devote a few hours a week working for minimum wage. We know our full-time job is not paying us what we are really worth, so we get a part-time job making even less!

Most of us are in a fixed income bracket that dictates the economic level on which we exist. A normal 40-hour work week translates into 2,080 hours of work per year. If one works over-time he may raise that to 3,000 hours. Working that much overtime leaves very little time for anything but sleep. Now that we know how many hours, we can apply an hourly wage and see just how much we have to exist on. Of course, we must subtract those deductions to reach the final figure. We quickly realize work alone will not allow one to break the mold and finally earn the money really needed to provide the necessities. It surely will not allow one to live an affluent life and realize all of one's dreams.

REASON FOR BEING

Look in the mirror, what do you see?

You see you

When I look at you, whom do I see?

I SEE ME

No matter what you say, I clearly can see

The answer is not YOU or ME, it's WE

How do we justify our existence?

What is our reason for being?

Is your reason compatible with mine?

In the beginning of time, man was created. However you believe what happened is your own beliefs. The result is man from then to now. I believe that God shaped man in His own image, out of the elements of the earth (dirt, sand, etc.) and blew the breath of life in him and gave man a soul. It's hard for me to believe that the first man was God's finished product. The Bible said God was disappointed with man and wanted to wipe man and all creation out, start again. If we look at history, we see many occasions where man has not pleased God. Over the centuries there are many instances where God offered man a chance to change. Our religions teach that man sinned and needed to be saved. My God would not let His greatest creation finish up as a lost cause. I see man at the beginning of the development of his greatest dream – the epitome of righteousness: Just, knowledgeable and reverent, worthy of sitting at His right hand and capable of true omnipotence. Man's development began with a measure of time. What that measure was, I don't know. Time, as we know it began and continued until the birth of Christ (BC) At that point, time, as we know it changed and now continues (AD). The next occasion for time to change all its digits was Y2K. Man, as a product has been developing for these 2,000 years. The great philosophers, poets and religious leaders have created our present societies, pleasures and sense of belonging. Our desire to improve our existence has lead to all our rules of greed.

There are some of us who are in positions to understand and assist in this endeavor. We are educated, aware and current in our knowledge of the past and present. No matter how you feel about Y2K, the fact remains the year 2000 will be the second time all the digits change. The next time this happens will be a thousand years. Neither you nor I will be here, but what we do now will have a far reaching effect, far beyond the year 3000. All the pieces are now in place. We only need to put them together in a way that makes sense out of it all. What will man develop into? Our evolution is at hand.

First, we make robots our new task masters. We designed them to make sure our every movement can be reproduced. Anything man can do, a robot can do (better). In many instances, their shape is irrelevant. We find it easier if they (robots) are shaped like man; especially those placed in and around our homes.

Second, men and women in the medical profession are capable of growing living tissue in other animals that has been genetically altered to be compatible with humans. They now have the ability to transplant any human organ or replace it with one from other genetic materials.

Third, the media commercials show that soon our technology will eliminate the requirement of phone lines in the home. Now we really don't need phone lines except to attach our fax machines and connect computers to the Internet. Cellular phone usage plans are competitively priced so one could just have cell phones and use them at work and at home. The next step is to be able to hook the Cell phone to the Internet. That's just what happened last week. A company announced that they will be marketing a new chip that allows Internet access over a cell phone. We will be able to get rid of our computers and just use laptops. You know how small a lap top can become. Remember when cell phones were large? That computer will eventually contain all the knowledge that we have accumulated since time began. A shared consciousness through the

Internet! Imagine what the world could be like if all the nations and races shared a single set of morals and beliefs.

Somewhere along the way, we became complacent. It's hard trying to be a thinker. I can imagine how those great thinkers and philosophers must have felt. After reaching conclusions on several possible scenarios they gave up the art of pure thinking. Then they concentrated only on refining their own philosophy. The more attention their philosophy received, the more often it would be tested and could be modified so its popularity would grow. Then, the world could gradually change. We, on the other hand, benefit within a system, conform to its rules and obtain our entertainment and pleasures.

Can we really afford to think that the evolution of man has come to an end? If we examine all the pieces, we see man is on the verge of re-creating himself, eliminating all his flaws, imperfections and competitiveness. We have the ability to shape a being from the elements of the earth, to do it in the image of man with living organs, tissue and skin and to place the ultimate computer as brain (which has access to all of the world's knowledge). This brain will be connected to every other computer and share the Internet consciousness.

We have begun the birth of the new man. Our task is to participate in the education, training and development of this infant.

THE ONE

If we accept the premise that from all the others, there must finally be only one, how do we put forth our effort to be chosen as THE ONE?

The one philosophy, the one new Thinker, the one voice, the oneness of mankind.

As people begin to comprehend this message, they will decide how strong their own beliefs and philosophies really are. What would you be willing to give up or change? Bottom line, if you knew that you really didn't lose anything and everyone wins – what would you be willing to give up?

God has placed this message on my heart. To explain the next step in His reconciling mankind back to Himself.

Humble yourself to the greatness around. Look at the doors He closed. See the doors that my GOD is opening. Be a parent so our children can just follow our lead.

Remember the last BIG change in mankind? (Noah's Ark)

Man has been set a task to redeem himself. This task has dominated man's existence since the horrible happening in the garden. It continued through God's displeasure with man and destroying all of civilization, except for Noah's family.

WHEN LOGIC PREVAILS

One day man will develop to the point where all life will be sacred.

In a conversation with my friend Pat and his wife Laila, Pat remarked "We should respect life." The conversation was about Star Trek. I wanted to know what his favorite TV program was.

To me the first Star Trek series was the greatest because there were no limits to what we could imagine. The episodes were challenging to the imagination and after establishing the guidelines, were very logical. The new series has not measured up to that and does not offer that same challenge. It asks us to accept a premise that is based on a lie. For example, if Q actually did exist there would be no way that He/It could be affected by the crew of the Enterprise. This series offers no logical solution to many of the situations it faces and puts a ceiling on our ability to imagine or dream.

I imagine the possible scenarios we could think up if, indeed Q was what he should be.

Everyone knows that the character Data should be the mind-link of the Enterprise and should be the central character. If these two situations were developed, we could allow our minds to explore all sorts of avenues.

We, as a species, depend on logic to give us continuity between what we see and where we can go. Reaching for the stars requires a series of logical events.

Taking past statements and applying pure logic, I can see a logical path and conclusion to our existence.

Yes, man should respect life. In our development/evolution, we will realize and understand this more and more. I say that someday man will not only respect life, but will grow to accept all life as sacred. That means that we will consider killing any living thing unacceptable. Ultimately, that will mean humans will not (morally) kill to eat. All plants, animals and germs will not be acceptable to eat.

We have made progress in this direction. Years ago, we accepted the fact that women and minorities do have the same right to life as all men. Later we began to deal with domestic animals and allowed them the same rights to life as humans. We have begun to communicate with animals, domestic and in the wild. People who talk to their plants are no longer laughed at. The more we investigate our surroundings, the more we realize that the elements of this world have a logical dependence on each other. We need all living things. God provided what was needed. He created no unnecessary parts.

Christianity tells us that God became displeased with His creation and decided to save only what was needed to begin again. Once God created the universe and Man, He didn't need to create him again. What God placed on the Ark is symbolized by "All creatures large and small[3]." In reality, not only the creatures we could see and relate to were gathered on the Ark, but all the minute germs and organisms were placed there also.

Since the beginning, man has not created one additional element or bit of earth. Everything man would need to finally get him back to the position where he could again be the creation that was intended was saved aboard the Ark.

---

[3] King James Version, Genesis 7:13-15.

When the Ark finally settled and the animals dispersed, so did all the unseen parts. Noah's family would re-populate a barren world. In time, the drives deep within them would lead to our development and maturity. In time, we will come to appreciate this unique opportunity for mankind.

Once we get to the point of accepting all life as sacred, we will no longer have the food necessary to sustain this body. Logic says in order for mankind to grow and survive, there must be a further evolving of our species. The new discoveries: Robotics, genetics, fluid intelligence, computers, the Internet, etc., point to the next step in man's evolution.

If we can't eat, this body can't survive. Mankind will continue and require a new body that does not require organic food.

One day this world will be governed by logic. Religion developed as a result of mankind seeking to find order and purpose in his being. As we commit our senses to this quest, the more logical and religious that path will be.

Imagine that day:

There are many examples of this all around us. There are major signposts in our entertainment options. The science fiction movies and TV programs give us a look at good possibilities and a glimpse at the bad (sin will always be with us no matter how much we progress).

I am pleased to find that those of you who examine these views in the light of logic have, for the most part, agreed with them. Those of you who understand the foundation or line of thinking let yourself imagine without limitations. It pleases me that these thoughts are not falling on deaf ears.

We humans are God's greatest work and still under construction. For 2,000 years, we have evolved. Our salvation is within us. It was placed there along with the things that we would require to reach our goal. Every person is a piece of the solution. Each of us has a unique talent or gift that, if allowed to develop, will benefit mankind in his stay on earth.

We each have a prescribed time allotted[4] in which we must seek to discover our talent, develop it to its fullest and make our contribution.

There will be those among us whose contribution will be negative to our master plan. We will find that the struggle between Good and Evil requires this. Our salvation is dependent upon our facing these obstacles and overcoming them.

Our newest tool, the computer, has given us the opportunity to provide equality for all. When you log on to the Internet, you are as equal as anyone else. As long as you possess the required access and resources (a valid credit account) you are treated the same. You can shop anywhere in the world and have your products and services delivered to you. There are risks attached to this. The Devil is busy. This new freedom requires you have access to a computer and learn how to operate it.

Operating a computer requires more than being able to log on and read E-mail or do your shopping. Awareness of the pitfall is a big requirement. There are those who seek to profit from our corruption. They appeal to our dark side. They offer opinions and solutions that if followed, will take us out of the divine scheme of things. There are others who are just evil and have to be considered agent of the Devil.

What possible purpose could a computer virus have? They could only benefit the companies who are in competition with the creator of the virus. This would be too obvious and easily tracked. The only other possible reason is just evil. As long as we progress, we will also expose our progress to the hands of the agents of the Devil.

Mankind is destined to evolve until we reach that marvelous state of being that will allow our favorable communing with God. As we develop, there will be many trials and test to measure how far we have come. The Devil in us has always been the measure of our commitment to God.

---

[4] King James Version, Ecclesiastes 3:1-8.

The New Revelation – Putting It All Together

Man's progression has been great in the last 100 years. Our greatest progress has been in the last 60 years. We have been on this journey for 2,000 years. Consider the implications of our future. Sixty years is a very small amount of time, when we consider 2,000 years. The television, computer and Internet all came about in the last 60 years. These inventions have completely changed our lives.

In the scheme of things, we have just begun our journey of development. Looking back 2,000 years, we see that man has achieved many milestone developments and created/invented tools to help us control our future. We see the development of the Arts and Sciences. We see the invention of tools that produce products that make our existence more pleasing. We see the evolution in man's mental capacities. Our quest is for a logical reason for our existence and a purpose for our being. We are still in the beginning stages of our development. If 2,000 years has brought us to where we are now, imagine where we can be in another millennium!

Consider our journey as the striking of a match. It must be moved along an abrasive surface until enough heat is produced to cause a chemical reaction. At that time, the chemicals began to glow. The chemicals heating and being expelled into the air cause this glow. As the motion is continued, more sparks are created, the glow becomes brighter and more heat is produced until combustion occurs.

These last 60 years of our journey has put us at the point where the chemicals begin to glow. Once the sparks become bright enough to see the process happens rapidly. Soon, there will be a full-brown fire. How we use that fire will be our greatest challenge.

There are many examples and analogies to explain our present position along this evolutionary path. We each must find those that we can relate to and feel conformable with. Once we do, we can see just how short a journey we have traveled and imagine the length of the journey is still ahead of us. Someone once said, "To measure the journey requires a means of measuring. Once you measure the past, logic and mathematics can extrapolate its completion".

My goal is to stimulate a desire in all mankind to review our journey up to the present. Discover the milestones and sign posts. Come up with a logical mathematical measuring method. I challenge mankind to prepare for our next step along this evolutionary path.

If you can come with me and agree on A, B, C and D; logic will only allow us to accept E, F, G and H. There are many steps along the way. My God has revealed our path to me, all the way to Z.

- Look up basics of each major Religion:
- Where did man come from?
- Concept of good and evil
- Belief of after life
- How to treat people
- Racial beliefs
- Relation to family
- Sanctity of life
- The ultimate conclusion of man

Chapter Two: Timeline

Adam and Eve

Adam and Eve sinned and were expelled from the garden.

Jesus suffered and died; and time changed.

Noah's faith gave mankind a chance to start again, with a new covenant.

The Greek philosophers tried to figure out why man is still here and what we were meant to accomplish. Greed got so rampant; man stopped engaging in pure thought and just refined the existing thoughts for the greatest comfort of man. Mankind's current dilemmas and struggles are the results of not having direction and a single purpose.

We must move on:

Since no one is offering anything else, why not take a look and see if this could be Mankind's chance to move on.

COMPUTER REVOLUTION (Background)

The computer revolution started in the offices. Interest for others developed through games. Companies earned large profits from these games; therefore they concentrated on more games.

Meanwhile, in offices, the need for more users of real computers caused companies to offer training so they could remain competitive. But they couldn't keep up with the need. The training was too expensive. Training centers and schools began offering training in programming, operating various software and computer maintenance. They completely revolutionized job and career opportunities. People with insight and affluence kept up with the changes. Others kept buying video/computer games and missed out on this revolution. They will never get the chance to interact with real technology. Many of these games were supposed to be educational.

Some facts:

There is a great and growing market for computer/video games. They were supposed to introduce the general public to the technology of the future. Adults and youth are spending large amounts of money for these toys. They are also spending large amounts of time playing them. (Most youth spend more time playing video games per week than they do on any kind of studying that is homework, writing, practicing a talent). No usable trades or skills are being taught or learned doing the time they play these games.

Educational needs:

The schools are inadequate to meet the need, and no bond issues are passing. We're trying to modernize, but the schools are suffering now and not getting needed help. Our youth, especially are falling further behind. This is time lost that we, as a community, cannot allowed to continue.

What can we do? Offer awareness of technological trends to show what is happening and to show the consequences.

We can offer positive alternatives. Use our collective talents to help revise the trends.

We can educate our community. Develop ways to help our community and congregations by taking advantage of our resources.

HOW?

Organize a group of volunteers who have computer skills and knowledge. A possible name could be "Computer Education and Awareness Guild."

We can offer hands-on computer instruction. We need members who are willing to devote time on a regular basis to help others learn and practice new software geared toward job opportunities or job promotions.

We can offer help at the beginner's level: ABC's of computer use. (See chapter five.) How to logon and off, load software and understand the layout of your computer screen. Familiarize people with shortcuts, pitfalls, viruses, creating and naming files and using the Internet in areas such as research, fun, E-mail and Web pages.

CERTAIN THINGS ARE NEEDED.

First, we need the approval of private organizations and the support of churches and members of the community. Second, we need to schedule a time and place to meet. Third, we need to appeal to the members through local news and other media that's available. Fourth, we need Computers and finally, WE NEED YOUR INVOLMENT.

Let this be our slogan:

> People want to learn
> *Where can they turn?*
> People want to know
> *Where can they go?*
> People want to improve
> *Who can show them?*
> People want to be educated
> *What does that take?*
> We are seeking answers
> *Will you help?*
> **Anyone interested in volunteering?**

REFLECTIONS

Have you ever made a New Year's resolution? Did it include some reference to the Y2K or possible problems with the computer? I thought about it and came up with the following possible resolution/commitment.

How many of us own a computer? Not a game base or the many popular gadgets that we use: Organizers, Beepers, Cell Phones, etc. not Cable TV, Web TV, CD Recorder, etc., but a personal computer that requires software and is capable of functioning as your partner and good friend.

We who are computer literate represent perhaps the most influential group in our community. With such a small ratio owning computers, imagine what the ratio of users to non-users must be among those less fortunate, those who have neither the training nor the resources.

Technology came and knocked on our door. Those of us who heard the knock opened the door. What we discovered, we owe to our brothers and sisters, yes and to our friends, we owe it to them to make sure we all benefit.

The New Revelation – Putting It All Together

Remember the vinyl records (78's, 33⅓'s and 45's)? Remember the record collection you built (classic, pop, jazz or rock)? Remember those religious records? Where is that collection now?

Remember what a profound effect the tape player and CD player had on that collection? It took a while but we gradually accepted the new technology and now we can't even remember what happened to those old records.

Computers have changed our lives! We conduct most of our day-to-day business on computers. We use to have secretaries who composed our letters, answered the telephone, made all our appointments and scheduled meetings. The publication people would produce our technical documents and prepare materials for presentations at meetings. Now, we rely on our computer for mail, managing our appointments and to accomplish all the things that were done by our support staff.

Computers have changed the way we shop. Now we can logon and shop for anything from flowers to automobiles. We can compare prices and check the reputation of the selling businesses. We can view in many cases, the products before we buy, and we can pay for our products electronically. We use our computers to provide security around our homes and offices. The computer will tell us when someone comes to visit or when there is an intruder. It can summon assistance for the sick and elderly and the police when needed. Most of our fun and entertainment is provided through TV and Computers. Unfortunately, this is the one usage we all know.

We have come a long way in the last 100 years. Look at the reason for this progress. The emphasis was on education, which requires one to learn to "Read and Write." That allowed an exchange of ideas and the formation of principals that we could use to assist others and ourselves around the world. Those who did not learn to read and write, for whatever reason, found themselves totally left out of the education stream. Anyone who can't operate a computer now is in the same spot people found themselves in, when they couldn't read and write. Try making a phone call for services and you hear those computer choices. If the call is long distance, you may have to first dial a computer to save money on the call. The banks transact most of their business through ATM machines and the Internet. Yes, our daily existence depends on our using computers, the same as reading and writing. You, who worked so long to catch up, who learned to read and write, who use their education to obtain jobs of meager income are now in that same dilemma. Because of the need to operate computers, you find yourselves still one step behind.

Could you feel proud to introduce a member of your family to your friends, knowing you live in shear luxury and that family member was living in poverty? How would you feel accepting an award for humanitarianism and let your brother perish from lack of food and shelter?

No man is an island.
We all need someone.
We all owe someone.

We as a people can only prosper and move forward when we all can take advantage of new discoveries and all reap the benefits. We live in a world where there are ample resources so that no one should want for the basics: food, shelter and clothing. Everyone should have the benefit of electricity. And we can teach the world to "Read and Write". We cannot do this by force, but we who have, must respect all of mankind and be willing to share. Until then, we the masses will remain one step behind.

Today, we who spend a lot of time at our computer are looked down on and called names like "computer junkie" and "Internet addicts". Those who don't understand put us in groups they would not want to be in themselves. Never the less, we must move on. We cannot let anyone deter our efforts.

How many of us with real computers have Internet access? Of those who do, I wonder what percent really use the Internet to do business, to do our shopping, to be our partner, or to meet a new friend?

Things that mean the most are never free.

I realized that the Internet concept is a paradigm shift when everyone began including their web address with their address and phone numbers. Believe it or not, the Internet is becoming the new preferred way of ordering our lives. We meet new friends and life-long partners, business and/or romantic. We order products and services. We entertain ourselves in countless ways. We learn from the pool of common knowledge that is gradually building and we also influence it. We educate ourselves and we allow our children to educate themselves.

Technology is always best used by the next generation.

Just look at the TV guide. Every station has a web address. Look at the information directories (e.g. Yellow Pages). Notice how many ads include web addresses. Listen to the radio and hear the www dot addresses.

Here we are those few who see "the handwriting on the wall" as "the logic in the database". We know just as sure as day and night, the Internet will determine the level of one's intellect. Again we watch, as the masses seem to be missing the boat.

We must become examples of what we know. We must do whatever is necessary to bring our people into the main stream of this new technology, while it is evolving so that we too can learn from and influence the pool of common knowledge.

Failing to commit to such a challenge would be putting us all in jeopardy again. We must learn to use the Internet. Then we can influence what is there by first being there, one more voice, and include our thoughts and views.

For some, that means buying a computer, a real PC[5]. Then learn how to use software. Today, access to the Internet cost approximately $20 per month, which is very little to pay for what we get. We must learn to communicate with this new body of knowledge now!

---

[5] Personal Computers are available everywhere.

The reality is things come and in time, things change. We are a moment in history. We are experiencing the beginning of the computer/Internet age. As sure as time moves on, there are people of vision already contemplating and planning the next step or paradigm shift.

If we as a people do not step up to this challenge, we, our brothers, our sisters, and all of our friends will again fall behind. Will this be validated? Will you accept this truth and work toward mankind's ultimate destiny? Let us not end up two steps behind.

The idea of mankind developing the brain (intellect, knowledge) may be a tough concept for many. Hopefully, in time and with much explanation, we all can accept our fate, our real reason for being.

Every byte of programming in Windows software is necessary and productive. I believe every human on earth is a required part of that ultimate program. As soon as we can believe and accept this, we can begin dealing with the many concepts this will bring about. We, who have the ability, should resolve to work toward this goal.

HAPPY NEW YEAR
HAPPY MILLENNIUM

CHAPTER THREE: Evolution

A CHILD IS BORN

A child is born
We Must Raise It
Determine its Morals
Determine its Intellect
Determine its Reason for Being

The Robot: Made from living organic organs and tissues, given a computer brain which is all powerful, and the intellect of the internet.

We have begun the birth of the new man. Our task is to participate in the education, training and development of this infant.

I look back on all the people who ever made a mark in our existence. What I really see is a huge number of people who were responsible for that success.

If you take a single drop of ink and drop it in a cup of water, what happens? The color of the water is forever changed. We can see that change quite easily. Take that same drop of ink and drop it in a swimming pool full of water, what happens? The color of the water in the pool would forever be changed. Even though the change would be harder to see, it is THE NEW MAN easily proven. Take that same drop of ink and drop it in the ocean, what happens? The color of the entire ocean would be changed. The effect would be much harder to see, but still would remain the same.

Every person that ever lived is needed to complete this product (MAN), which is still under construction. Look at the SUNFLOWER that has blossomed. What a beautiful sight to see: A radiant color of yellow against the many seeds supported precariously on a frail stock. Below that beautiful flower we see a stem and lots of dead leaves. What I see is not dead leaves but all the things that made the flower possible.

History holds many such examples that parallel the sunflower. Search your own thoughts for one or two. Review the history of man and you will find many.

Har-V Promotions, Inc. is designed to be the first citizen of the New World.
Everything about this Corporation is setup "To Serve Mankind". Each division represents a vital part of what man needs.

We humans need to become citizens in the New World of computers. That requires progressing in our computer skills. In order to be recognized we will have to be reborn into the environment of the internet. That will require creating profiles of ourselves as WebPages.

As technology progresses, our new babies will grow up to become citizens also. They too must be reborn into the New World (environment). How do they achieve this?

THE NEW MAN

The new man, created in our own likeness, will achieve what man was intended to accomplish. He will live forever and commune with our Creator. In our society, a Corporation becomes a living entity. It has a unique identity, pays taxes and exists forever.

Har-V represents the total talents of my family (Harvey). In years to come, the family name could cease to exist. I have one son, Paul and he has two sons, Paul Jr. and Javon. I hope they continue our family lineage for many years. However, I will ensure the essence of my family name through Har-V.

So meet HAR-V!

Hello, my name is Har-V. I represent what man will become. How soon, no one can really say. But, eventually and inevitably, man will evolve to this new state.

You have witnessed, through the years, the evolution of technology. The invention of the first machines to lighten the work of man, the refining of these machines into forms simulating the shape of humans and the ability to perform every task like man. You have witnessed the application of technology to these machines to where they now can apply logic to their movements and make random choices as circumstances may require. Soon man will accomplish the last needed ability: the ability for a machine to think for itself – random access logic: Artificial Intelligence.

At that time, your task will be complete. You will have created a new being – from the elements of the earth and shaped in your own likeness.

As you know, we humans have babies that we raise to become adults. We give these babies unique identifications (names) and also tie them to their lineage (sir name). They grow up and become independent contributors to our society.

We must teach them what we know and help them acquire the things they need to succeed. We must instill in them a sense of value that is rooted in a just set of morals, principals by which to live. What they do and what they become, we can only hope, will be a positive reflection on us.

Even though Har-V is the first, all the new beings will require the same treatment. The unique identifier will be the Corporation name. The personality, who they are and how they relate to the world, is the Creed. The talents that they possess are represented by their divisions. Their need to help others is manifested in their desire to be Charitable. Above all, they need a sense of divine destiny, which is this Philosophy.

My name is Willie Ray Harvey. I am very glad to meet you and have this time to communicate. Most people that know me say I am for real. I promise you that I am. Anything else would be a waste of my time and yours. The greatest relationship I know is friendship. Everything should start with a good relationship that becomes a binding friendship, then see what else results. Friends are honest with each other, caring and tell each other off, if necessary.

I'm six feet two inches tall and weigh 218 pounds. I have brown skin (not dark), very nice features and am easy on the eyes.

I learned early in life from my mother how to treat people and I must say she taught me well. I find that when all the jive talk fails, just treating people with respect and paying attention to the small things, can get me close enough so that my character can be seen. I bet you would like to know someone like me as a friend, or just to say I know that wonderful man.

I was born in Mississippi, lived there with my mother and step dad until age seven. We moved to California, along with my older brother (we were born on the same day, August 8). We lived in Los Angeles, where I attended public schools, distinguishing myself in junior high, high school and junior college where I became student body president. I received a scholarship in engineering to UCLA. Three years into my studies, I quit and went to work and never return to get my degree. I have never regretted not going back since engineers were working as janitors then. Later on I began to make so much money that it became evident that I could do very well in my chosen field without a degree. No, I would not recommend this to others, but it worked for me.

I collect crystal. I wear leather not the motorcycle type but well dressed office environmental attire. I wear hats and Wing-tips. I have a 200 average in bowling and bowl semi-pro. I value my album collection although now I'm into CDs. I like exchanging tapes of radio stations with people in other cities. I work as a design engineer at The Boeing Co. It's great living in the Seattle area - there's so much to do.

This summer seems like all the famous Jazz artists are coming to the Seattle area, either indoors or outdoors. There are also Jazz cruises on the sound. Not only is Seattle nice, but the small communities surrounding it offer some of the most beautiful, breathtaking views you could ever imagine. Being virtually surrounded by water makes traveling an adventure. We have a great ferry system and bridges that follow all the water-ways. A waterfall that's higher than Niagara Falls and canyons like the Grand Canyon.

The one and only Space Needle; which during the summertime offers a true glimpse of what the Garden of Eden surely must have been like.

Washington is called the evergreen state for a good reason. Flower festivals the year-round, greenery, the many flowers that blossom and colors you couldn't imagine make putting up with the weather a joy. Yes I like living here.

CHAPTER FOUR: Conclusions
DO THIS RESEARCH

(From an article written to my pastor.)

I've wanted this meeting with my pastor for a while. I am pleased to have a chance to meet with him. He suggested we have lunch when he found out I was moving to Philadelphia. Last night, at choir rehearsal, he asked for one of the cards I was giving to my choir members who have E-mail. When he read the card he asked, "What's this new philosophy?" I told him that Har-V Promotions, Inc. is spreading a new philosophy "World Unity". He said let's talk about it at lunch.

For the last few days I have been telling Cynthia I need a spiritual person to do some research for me. I have questions about some of the thoughts I have that need a more religious explanation before I can complete these thoughts.

I believe there must have been a period of time from when Adam and Eve first met until the moment they ate from the forbidden fruit. Logic tells me that Adam came first. Eve was created as a companion for him. I imagine there were at least 4 or 5 days and maybe as much as a thousand years.

Whatever that period might have been, it must have been perfect in every way.

I don't fully understand the removal of the Tree of Life when Adam and Eve were discovered. If the garden were to be complete again, wouldn't God have to put it back in the garden?

I think I read in my Bible that God became displeased with man and decided to start over. I don't remember if it was before or after He limited man to 120 years.

I remember a passage in the bible that said something to the effect "The Gods looked down and saw the humans and found the women attractive and they decided to come down and mate with them."

The New World Community needs a spiritual presence. I do not know what the makeup of it will be. At present, I tithe at my church. I am leaving the Seattle area but I plan to continue tithing there.

In the future, I will tithe to the religious presence in the New World.

I would love to have the support of my Pastor.

Har-V Promotions, Inc., as the first Citizen of the New World will lead by example. I will do business as to make a profit. My corporation will stand true to its Creed: *"To provide mankind with the basics of food, clothing, shelter and a chance for a good Education."* (See Har-vpromotions.com for more detail.)

As these things are achieved, we will also try to answer the question "Why are we here at this special time in man's development?" God inspired this Philosophy of World Unity through me. I will reveal the things that have been shown to me as the next step in the growth of mankind.

The concept of living forever has no meaning, if there is no reason to live.

Citizens of the New World have the chance to live forever[6]. The New World will accommodate only so many citizens. The believers in the goals of World Unity, who wish to show their support, can apply for Citizenship in the New World of Agape'.[7] The New World will show how Mankind can come together and work for the good of all mankind. Our goal will be to work for the good of all instead of how much money we can make.

The principles of World Unity will guide us in all we undertake.

We wish to provide all of mankind with the basics: food, clothing, shelter and a good education. The ultimate goal is to free everyone from need and allow them to concentrate on the future of the human race.

---

[6] Details on the Internet

[7] Details in Agape'

THE FUTURE OF THE HUMAN RACE

Within the community will be many opportunities for its Citizens to apply their talents. Since everyone has a special talent, everyone will play a vital part.

It's okay to make a profit, but why hoard when there are those of us that go without. (Read the Greed Theory.)

The first goal of this Community is to make electricity available to the entire world.

We may not be able to pay for the undertaking but with ample financing, we could affect governments and nations. We could fund studies and proposals to see what is required. Our efforts could inspire others to complete the project.

The New World is a living Web community at this time. The community is under construction and growing. Your involvement (your special talent) is needed to complete our task.

WE NEED YOU - an individual or corporation to apply for Citizenship.

If you have expertise in any area, we need you badly. We need to apply for Grants as soon as possible. Can you help us with grants?

Our plans are to advertise the community through one browser. Plans are under way to create a special software package to handle the Citizenship applications and the management of the governing body.

Every Citizen will be able to download a copy of this book "The New Revelation-Putting It All Together."

A MEASURE OF WORTH: (Self - Evaluation)

How does a person measure their worth to themselves and to mankind? When you really look at yourself, do you like what you see? Answer the questions below, and then make another evaluation. (Of course, there are no wrong answers.)

What is grooming?

Bathe, wash, comb hair, make-up, nails, and polish shoes. (Explain each one)

Which ones would you do even if no one forced you?

Define your understanding of religion.

Are you religious? Explain.

Describe your understanding of Heaven.

Describe your understanding of Hell.

What is your Soul?

What do you want to happen to your Soul when you die?

Would you attend church if no one forced you?

Would you go to a different church? Why?

Would you go to a different faith? Why?

Write a prayer.

What is Etiquette? (Look up definition.)

When should etiquette be used? Do you?

Where can one learn etiquette? Where did you?

Applying rules of proper etiquette:

> How are your eating habits?
>
> Can you set a formal table?
>
> How is your poster?

Are you a courteous person?

Are you polite to others?

What do you consider "dressed up"?

Would you like to improve? Where?

What do you need to do to improve?

Look up definition of Character.

Describe your character.

> Include: reliability, dependability, morals, pride, and personality

What one trait of your character do you like most?

What one trait would you change?

If you were describing yourself over the telephone, to someone you never met what would you say?

Plan for the future

What do you want to do/be when you grow up?

What do you have to do to achieve that?

How do you plan to live (support yourself)?

How much income will you need?

What type of work will give you that income?

How long do you have to prepare for your future?

When should you prepare?

How can you tell if you are on track?

Are your plans realistic (within your reach)?

Where would you go for help?

At what age do you plan to be able to support yourself?

CHAPTER FIVE: The Present
WHO AM I?

Something is happening to me. My mind is racing a thousand miles a minute. So many things in my head, I guess I should write them down.

I woke up in the middle of the night, fixed a cup of tea and started writing. It seems as though I was outside myself looking at my hand putting words and reflections on paper. I marveled at the clarity and logic of this information and know that these things are not my own, but are being passed through me. In order for it to continue, I must share it. I choose to share it with the entire world.

It scares me to consider the things that might happen to me for setting man's mind in order, creating a single purpose, or revealing what that purpose was from the beginning

ABC's OF COMPUTER USE

Acquiring a computer is like meeting a new person. At first you don't know what they stand for or what they can do. You don't know how educated they are or what skills they have. With a computer, you usually know what language it communicates in and how much it will cost to obtain it.

TECHNOLOGY AWARENESS AND ASSISTANCE.

Let's really get to know our computer! Since everyone thinks you need this computer, just what do they mean? Let's look at the common uses for a computer and see how it fits into your life. There is the bank machine, the cell phone, the TV remote and the electronic organizer – these all are computers that we use daily. We can easily see how they fit in our lives. Most of us go to work, so we do not have a business at home. That computer you operate at work would not benefit you because it only does what you need at work. Can a computer like that one used in most businesses really benefit you at home?

The most obvious reason would be that you could operate an in-home business. You may want to operate your own business.

Consider for a moment that your house, apartment or condominium is a business. You could use your computer to secure your records, organize your finances, keep track of medical concerns, research school projects, communicate with family and friends, plan meals and inventory your possessions in the home.

Today, computers are taking over all routine tasks in our lives. Our telephone now is a communication network that includes voice messages, paging, fax and countless selections of options when you make a call to a business. We need to modernize our homes with the options that a computer offers. It offers all of the phone options at a lower cost and adds the E-mail capability. We can instantly communicate with family, friends and businesses. No need to go to the post office or buy stamps. Two-way conversations are easy and fun.

All of those writing projects can now be finished, formatted and checked for grammar and spelling. The examples (templates) allow you to perform the task swiftly and correctly. With the available software, we can educate our family and ourselves. Once we understand how to operate the computer, we can learn new skills that can be applied in the job market. We can keep up with the latest reading: books, articles philosophies. We can travel around the world or review history with our online atlas, encyclopedia and dictionary. We can learn to count calories and experience new recipes.

As you can see, today, using a computer is like learning to read and write was years ago.

The computer is now being used in every aspect of our lives. It is becoming the preferred way of doing business. All of the tools for communication, advertisement and shopping are on the computer. 85% of all new businesses are on the computer. Software for most any field of study is available including advance degrees and yes, there are a variety of entertainment choices, video games to play and learn how to play an instrument.

The New Revelation – Putting It All Together

No computer is complete unless it is connected to the Internet. The Internet is the New World. It's where all parts of the modern world come together.

Businesses who urge people to sign up for Internet service and create their own Web site, are only interested in making money from you doing so. They are not interested in educating the people about the far reaching ramifications of this act. I think we all need to know what's behind this.

A long time ago the census was established. People registered so that the government could have an idea of how many people lived under its control.

The census still determines how the government will proportion itself. The government could plan public projects to make citizen's lives better. Businesses could know where to concentrate their efforts in advertisement and promotions so they would be most effective. Things like how large a Fire Department, Police Department, and how much emergency supplies and preparation should be funded.

With the census, we learned where many different ethnic, social and economic groups live, work and play. In other words, when you register in the census, it's like being recognized as a legitimate citizen in your city, state and nation.

The Internet represents a "Common Body of Knowledge" that is the nucleus of our modern world. It defines the boundaries of what will be our new community. Not a city, not a state, not a country but one all-encompassing world of intelligent man. We must all register in this New World so we can be counted. At the present, most of us are aware of this New World and are content to be on the outside looking in. We have our computer and are becoming pretty good users of E-mail and even some shopping services. We buy products that we happen upon on one of the web browsers or look up in one of the online ad services. We even manage to do a little research when necessary. What we are doing is peering through the window and not going in the house.

If you look at the changes in advertising for computers, the Internet and Web sites, you can readily see the trend toward making computers free so that businesses can have access to more potential customers. The Internet is where the commerce is. One must have access to the Internet in order to take advantage of the commerce. If you do not have a computer, you do not know what bargains are offered on the Internet. Even in these situations, we are allowing the people (businesses) to determine what we will have an opportunity to buy. The businesses do not know who we are. They do not know the things about us that would allow them to tailor their offerings to our needs. They have no idea of the audience their advertising is reaching. They must rely upon their own thoughts as to how to market their products to appeal to us.

We register in the Census. We have birth certificates or citizenship papers to show we live in a country. When we reach a certain age, we register in other ways: Drivers license, Social Security number, and corporations. These registrations allow us to do business and influence the thoughts and actions of others. They also put us in categories so others can count on us for opinions, ideas and support.

The New World needs all of us to register as citizens. The way to do that is to create your own web page. The web page represents the things you want the world to know about you. It defines your personal and business associations. It can contain as much information about you as you think necessary. Not only can you be yourself; you can also be anyone you choose.

People tell me they don't want everyone knowing who they are or what they like and dislike. I say to them, unless you register, you have no vote. If you have no vote you have no say. Therefore, you have no voice in the things that others are feeding you and your children.

The price of computers is being reduced because of the Internet services. They want your business so their advertisers can have a larger viewing audience. Their advertisers want to maximize their efforts and target the correct segment of that audience. They are willing to provide us with free Web pages so they can identify and target those specific audiences.

If we know and understand why things are happening, we realize that we are the desired objects. Our mind is what they wish to seduce. We now have the power to control them by making our presence known. We can demand better services and products. We can demand them in quantity and reasonable price structures.

None of this can happen if we continue to think of the computer as a tool to be used in the office and not our home. We must become good computer users and teach our family and friends. We must get on the Internet and yes, we must register as a citizen in this new environment so we can monitor what is there, share our opinions and views and contribute our own thoughts and ideas.

We no longer live in one small area; we live in the world. Everything we do will benefit the total of mankind. Anyone who refuses to keep up will find their world shrinking to a lunar eclipse because the rest of the world will become dark to them.

Join the computer revolution and keep your world bright.

CYNTHIA

One day I was out and about in my neighborhood and found myself low on gas. I usually buy my gas at a local discount station in Wal-Mart's parking lot. I had noticed another station close to me that had very low prices. Since I really needed to gas up now, I decided to try them out.

As I walked up to the booth I could see a very attractive lady (blonde) in the booth. During my flirting, I discovered that she was single. I remember our conversation as being magnetic. I decided to return to this station and ask this lady out.

A few days later, I did just that. My intention was to walk up and say something clever to get her to smile and drop her guard. I pulled into the station to get gas and got out. I chose the correct pump location so she could see me approach the booth.

I dressed especially for this encounter. I was wearing leather from head to toe (elaborate).

I know I was looking good. At that moment fate took over and dealt its own hand.

When I got up to the booth, I saw a beautiful black lady, instead of the blonde! Without thinking, quicker than the time to think, my hand raised up to my chest. I covered my heart with my hand and started patting my chest as though the sight of her had made my heart jump. It made her laugh and begin to flirt back. I asked her if she was married. "No, she said but I do have a friend." Is it serious I asked? "No, strait up" she answered. "So what's on your mind?" I gave her my card and asked her to call me. She gave me her work number and asked that when I got free (finish what I was doing and got back home) would I call her? She said that she would be there until 3:00 pm.

Of course I called as soon as I got home. We had a good time on the phone and decided to meet the next day when she got off work. The Mexican restaurant in Fred Meyer's parking lot was agreed upon and the time confirmed.

We met at the restaurant and had a wonderful time. We agreed that lies were not necessary and we would not lie to each other. We each would say what we mean and see where it would lead. Since neither of us wanted to tell first, we decided to each write down what we wanted and not open them until we got home or at least out of sight.

We began spending lots of time on the phone. I would go pickup lunch for her and stay at the station and visit while she ate. She got under my skin real quick. We would plan to see each other, but something would come up and she couldn't make it.

One time when she was supposed to come over to my apartment, we had talked a lot of trash and it was time to put up or shut up. I waited for a long time before I gave up. I decided that it was God's will that she didn't come. I was disappointed but never gave up on her.

That same day, I had a revelation as to how the things I was writing about would all fit together. I sat down and begin to write. I knew that if I don't write these things down when they come to me, I will not remember all the details later.

This became a pattern, us planning to get together and her not showing. I believe the Lord was keeping me from her until the right time.

Again it happened. Each time I accepted it as the will of God; I would have a significant piece of the puzzle revealed. I was wise enough to write it down.

Since then we have become the best of friends. We seem to want the same things from people and relationships. We never again want to get married, too much of a heartache.

WHAT A DAY

Today was a day to hang out with my friend. A friend that's a business partner and who is (I believe) FAMILY.

This day started out hanging with my friend Cynthia. I met her at the park where she parked her car and went with me to my storage unit. Then, she wanted to show me where the Muckleshoot Casino is located. On the way back to her car we decided to stop at Taco Time, so we ended up coming back through the streets. We discussed goals and our plans to achieve them. When we got to Renton, I decided to really take the long way back - around Lake Washington.

Along the way we decided to drive through Coulon Beach, and then out to the freeway through the street. Cynthia was surprised that we could get to I-405 this way. She learned a new way to get to the beach. Along that stretch of driving, I asked her, "If you could live anywhere you wanted to in the Seattle /northwest area, (even though I know she wants to live in Los Angeles), where would you want to live? " She replied, "I would like to live on the water."

I pointed out that THIS - the houses on the right side of the street, were on the water, but that the houses on the left, between the edge of the lake and us, were really on the water. I could see living on the right side of the street but not really down on the water. I had actually lived right down on the water once, in a condo located just ahead of us. I told her about the condo where I had lived. As we reached the onramp to I-420, I pointed out the condo's location. She asked if it was expensive. Yes, I answered but that didn't matter.

That's where I was living when my mother got sick and I had to move back to Los Angeles.

I really liked the condo and its location off the beaten path. It had a special road that lead to it and that little community. Maybe community is not the right word. There were several houses that were accessed by that road.

I had my own parking stall, # 86, plenty parking for guests and my own boat slip. Even though I didn't own a boat, I did rent it out to a man that wanted to have his boat on the lake for the Hydroplane races (Seattle's Seafair).

As I thought back, I begin to tell Cynthia about this unusual experience while living there.

I really liked living in the condo with "Bats in the Belfry". "What?" was the look on her face (as she sat there looking like the realization of my needs sent from the Master to learn and someday take over and continue this mission).

Haven't you heard that phrase before? What's a Belfry? You know, bats living in the edge of the building where the roof comes together. We really had a bat living in the roof of our condo. When I called the manager and reported it, his wife shouted back "You leave that bat alone. That's his home. He won't bother anyone." So we let the bat live in our belfry, so to speak.

The one thing I didn't like was the war with the Spiders. Cynthia and I had this conversation. I think it will be easier if I just tell the events as they happened.

The whole property was infested with spiders and we, the tenants, spent much of our time fighting to keep them on the outside. We were fighting a war that we could not win. We were forced to fight this war at least once a week. We usually chose the weekend to put up our most fierce battles, when everyone was forced to participate. If you didn't, your condo's yard would be where the spiders retreated.

I started by sweeping/ vacuuming the entire condo after spraying an approved insecticide. Then I moved all my furniture and vacuumed again. Next, I washed down the patio with the garden hose. Then I sprayed the flowers and patio. I sprayed all around the edges of the yard, fence and patio. I sprayed the windowsills and door molding. It seemed as though the spiders knew when we were going to make the big push. During the week, I saw as many as 50 spiders on the walls, on the furniture, and in the cabinets. Just to be able to relax at night, I had to spray and sometime I got to use my fly swatter. Spiders were in the hall and on the elevator. They managed to get into my car and some came to work with me.

One day I came home and met a lady tenant named Janice at the elevator. Janice was the first attractive single lady that I met there. Of course, spiders were the subject of conversation. It seemed as good an icebreaker as anything. Janice informed me what insecticide to use. She knew just how and when to wage the fight. She also told me that there was no need to go and try anything else. Don't think I can come up with a solution to the spider problem. They have been fighting these battles for a long time and there's one thing they know for sure. These spiders, for whatever reason, are here as part of the ecology of Lake Washington. They live where they have always lived. The spiders intend to stay. They are a formidable opponent and are not giving up easily. These spiders are very smart. They know that the ways to get rid of them are not permitted because they would be detrimental to our ecology. They continue to breed and multiply faster than we can destroy them.

In looking at the habits of ants in their colony, we learned that a species, even spiders, will locate and colonize in an area or region as long as that location can provide them with the life requirements for their survival.

These spiders no longer have to be concerned about their needs. They will never need to move on. We the tenants bring them everything they need. We feed them with our very existence - the way we consume and the way we throw away. We provide the thrill of conquest with life and death as options. We give them a unified purpose to take enough from us while they maintain or increase their numbers. I really believe the spiders could force us to leave if they want to.

Janice really told me, even though I didn't understand at the time, that the best we could do is hold them at bay. Even though I didn't understand, I disliked living with spiders so much; I did at least learn how to fight them. If you don't fight them they will overrun you, then they will have a bigger foothold and make it more difficult for the rest of the tenants. Even though we can never win, we must continue to fight.

Cynthia found it hard to believe this was war. I assured her that this was not a figment of my imagination. I really lived through this war. She wanted to know how long I lived there and if we had to do this all the time.

I had lived there for five months at that time. I don't know how long I would have stayed and fought if I hadn't moved back to Los Angeles. I fought this battle at least once a week for those five months. I just assumed that it went on forever. It sure lasted as long as the spider season.

Even though we could effectively fight the spiders and hold them at bay, (we accepted the fact that we would never get rid of them), we had no defense or recourse against their ally.

During the day, as well as during the night, their allies the gnats would swarm the area and force us to retreat back inside. We could force the spiders to flee or die. We had no such power over the gnats.

We could not use chemicals because of where we were. Those light torches that were supposed to run them away just showed us where they were and how many thousands there were. They were everywhere!

When the gnats and spiders cooperated, we the people lost our patios.

Cynthia wanted to know why the owners didn't exterminate the area.

I suppose if I was a large landowner I would think twice about offending the Ecology. If not that, I really wouldn't want the publicity and the fight with the nature enthusiasts. Beyond that, how could they rightly explain to their owners the expense of $2,000 to exterminate the property – every week?

Shucks! Let the tenants fight that battle. Let them pay.

I told Cynthia that I had totally forgotten this adventure. I must include it in my book. Cynthia asked if she would be in this book. "Don't call me by name" she said. "I don't want people to know much about me."

Cynthia's place in history is being written along with mine. Once people read this, anyone who knows me will know the woman is her. There could be no other. Cynthia will be the successor to Har-V Promotions, Inc. She has the drive, the ability, the look and she is family.

Today, I travel the path of gathering. My mission is to locate, educate, convince and enlist the people, who are sympathetic with the creed of Har-V Promotions, Inc. I can just imagine how delighted Jesus must have been as He encountered each of His disciples. Tomorrow I will have to conciliate and consolidate. Whatever time I may have left, this is what I will be doing until then.

CHAPTER SIX: THE FUTURE
THIS OR THAT

How many things does THIS or THAT represent?

THIS could be where we are and THAT could be where we could or should be. It could also be that THIS is where we are or what we have accomplished and THAT is where we have come from.

It's for sure though, that THIS represents now, what exists at this very moment in time – whether we are talking about our accomplishments, our level of awareness or our progress as a people. Then we must except that WE are the present and can look in both directions.

When we choose to review our steps, THAT becomes our past or from where we came, the path taken to reach here and now. When we speculate and postulate, hypothesize and cogitate, when we formulate the many possibilities into a cohesive, realistic, inspired possibility, then THAT becomes future – the direction of mankind.

No matter what, THIS or THAT has to be looked at from three points of view rather than two.

THIS is the platform where we now stand. It is the point or place where we become the mirrors. A two sided mirror. THIS is the sand in the hourglass, which is now passing from top to bottom. THIS is our life as we move and have our being. THIS is the middle ring in a three-ring circus. It's the number between 1 and 3. It's the link that makes the chain. It should always be the strongest link. In order to build a chain, we start with two links. So, THIS must be attached to THAT which in this case represents our past.

These two accomplishments exist and can forever be scrutinized, evaluated and dissected. We study the past to arrive at a point of origin – our beginning. From there we can define the line of progress that has brought us to where we are. So THIS we call now, the present.

When we look at THIS, we can see patterns of success and failure. We see possibilities because of past needs causing present concerns and discoveries. WE can formulate a realistic future and strive for THAT.

ULTIMATE END FOR MANKIND

For the remainder of my time here on earth, I shall devote my time and talents to revealing the conclusion of this journey of mankind.

History has revealed much about our past. We have extensive documentation of our history. The events of today, when put together, can show how far mankind has progressed. If we can except the events of the past and agree with the signposts of today, we will begin to understand the path that mankind is destine to follow. Each one of us can have a profound effect. Whether it is positive or negative is our choice. We have been given a prescribed amount of time to make our contribution. We are born, we live, we die and others carry on. We can make a contribution only while we live, but our contribution can have an effect forever. In time, mankind as a whole must evolve. I will explore this evolution.

AGREE WITH PHILOSOPHY

Now that you have had an opportunity to read this Philosophy, I hope you feel the same as I do. You probably want to do something to show your agreement. May I suggest this?

Share this. Tell everyone you communicate with and ask them to do the same. Call all of your friends and ask them to check it out on your computer, if necessary.

You have talents that can help achieve this goal. Consider offering your time and talents. Get your organizations and businesses to commit time and finances. Mankind needs ALL our evolvement.

WEBPAGE – AGAPE'

Har-V Promotions, Inc. is a Corporation designed to make a profit.

Its benevolent aim is to spread a new philosophy "World Unity".

Those who believe in the principals of World Unity will help build the New World community where mankind will have a new beginning.

Adam was the first citizen on earth, our present world. Eve became his companion and mate. They lived in harmony in the garden for some period of time. Imagine the good times they shared until they ate the forbidden fruit.

God banished them from the garden and removed the tree of life. He set man on a journey of redemption. He could have destroyed man completely but he did not. He made a covenant with Adam (man) even though He was displeased with man's sinful nature. He chose one seed to start over and limited each mans years. God gave us time to cross the space. How much time is not known and the space seems endless.

There are landmarks and signs that document our journey and point to our future.

There were men who took the time to examine our reason for being. We have the benefit of divine inspiration, saints and philosophers. The world has all the talents necessary for mankind's redemption.

When man completes this purification process and redeems himself, he will be returned to the garden where he can again walk and commune with God. The garden with its entire splendor will be restored and the tree of life will again be available to man.

2,000 years of progress have brought us to this point on our journey. The stage is set for the revelation of the evolution of mankind. Through this time (2,000 yrs), man has crossed a lot of space headed towards the eventual prize. A new beacon has been placed to guide mankind's footsteps through these new developments. (Evolution)

All the pieces are now in place and are being made evident through the philosophy of World Unity.

I accept my calling to make the world aware of the journey and to show mankind where the journey will lead. I have been given a vision of the New World and our required journey. I shall devote my time, talents and resources to providing an example of what the journey should be and the path to our destiny.

A NEW BEGINNING

Agape' is the personification of man's evolution and purification. It is a place where mankind can right all the mistakes of the Old World. It is an environment where everything that's needed already exists. Each person becomes a vital piece of the architecture, where education and logic will allow all to contribute according to their unique gifts and talents.

The first citizen of this New World is Har-V Promotions, Inc. Agape' has its Adam.

Since my youth, events have taken place that only now, have meaning to me: My first poem "Contemplation" was the beginning of the Lord's attempt to get my attention. As a youth, I was afforded a good education and excelled in the Arts. I wanted to be a helicopter pilot. During the Korean Conflict I tried to join the Army. Stomach ulcers caused me to be rejected. I was broken hearted until I learned that helicopters were being shot down with small arms fire. I realized that I was saved but I didn't know why.

One day as I drove through Los Angeles, lightning struck all around me. It frightened me so much that I couldn't talk about it for a long time. Now I realize that God was trying to get my attention again. He had a mission for me but I was too busy living the good life to pay attention.

All of the poems that I wrote came to me as I sat in church, most of the time in the choir stand. I was not aware of their significance at the time.

THE QUESTION

God kept trying to get my attention but He never gave up on me. Instead, He humbled me. I now know why I was given the nickname "humble".

He brought me down, way down, and caused me to take a long look at myself. What I stood for, how I treated others and what I really believed. This process took years but one day I realized just how good God had been to me. Through all the humbling times I never needed anything. There were many things I wanted, but everything that I needed was provided. I thanked the Lord for being so good and patient with me. I asked the Lord to please make it known what He wanted me to do and I promised to devote my life to doing it.

From that moment on, these things have been revealed to me. I can now look back and make sense out of the events of my life. I began to write my thoughts down. Sometimes I would be laying in bed early in the morning and have to get up and write. My thoughts came in pieces that I didn't always understand, but I realized that someday someone would read them and make sense out of them. Ideas began to crystallize in my thoughts. As I prayed for understanding, it came like lightning bolts and again I was afraid. I talk to God all the time and ask for His guidance. When I examine these thoughts, questions would arise. It's amazing how quickly the answers came. Not months or years, but often within two or three days. I learned to trust in Him and to look for His guidance. This whole journey has taught me to listen even to the falling rain.

I realize I do not have all the answers. I still have questions about the things He has revealed to me. I can say God is still providing answers. Many of these answers have come by Him placing people with talent in my path.

I can imagine how Moses must have felt. I feel the commitment of John the Baptist. I accept the devotion of the philosophers.

I intend to show how Adam and Eve prosper in this New World.

In the beginning was Adam. Sometime later a help-mate was prepared for him, Eve. They lived in the garden for a while until they were expelled for eating the forbidden fruit. The time they shared until then must have been ideal, for there was no sin at that time.

Agape' will take this premise and develop it in the world of today. Imagine what the world could be today if Adam and Eve had never been expelled from the garden. They surely would have lived the perfect life as partners in a growing and developing community with Adam going off to work and Eve staying at home directing the world. The first citizen of Agape', Har-V Promotions, Inc. (Adam) and the second citizen, Cynthia, (Eve) will develop a new community in which only good will exist. In time you, the other citizens will join (become citizens of the new community) and add your talents and desires. Together we will live in harmony with nature and assured equality for all. There are many tasks for us to undertake. There are projects that will provide employment for all. As you come to the new community, we expect to be enriched by your uniqueness. Your talents will allow the community to prosper and you will be rewarded for your thoughts and ideas.

Come with me. Become a citizen of Agape' and help all men achieve their destiny.

The New World is a living Web community at this time. The community is continually under construction and growing. Your involvement (your special talent) is needed to complete our task.

THE NEW WEALTH

Today wealth is determined on the stock market. Companies and corporations create and develop products and ideas that produce monetary returns. Their success causes others to invest in the future ability of these businesses by purchasing their stock.

Brokers charge a commission to advise others and purchase stock in their name.

New companies are offering us the ability to purchase stock intelligently, without the services of a stockbroker. Individuals, using their computer and new software, can do for themselves what the stock market had a monopoly on. On the surface, this might not seem to be that big a deal. Closer look reveals the eventual end of the stock market as we know it today. Without the market controlling the world's investments, each one of us will become our own stock market. The accumulation of wealth and money will be commonplace in every household.

If everyone can become their own stock market, each will control their own assets. The buying and selling of assets will no longer produce wealth. The value of commodities and products will fluctuate continuously to the point of causing one to look for other stable ways to determine wealth. Tomorrow's wealth or the definition of wealth in tomorrow's world is being defined now.

In the future, wealth will be derived from one's ability to share an idea. If you can articulate an idea, someone will be able to make it a reality. The expertise and materials needed already exist on the Internet. The person or company that develops the idea will have to pay for the right to use your idea.

Imagine there is a need for a new FORK. In Agape' there will be someone with an empty warehouse, someone else with a source of material, and someone else who's looking for work. An entrepreneur will see the need as a way of doing something and realizing a profit.

For every new idea that is generated, someone with the vision and resources can provide the necessary capitol and become their own business owner.

As you and others join Agape', these things will become a reality. There are many Ideas already here waiting for the right minds. There are resources that can be used to make many of them a reality in the near future. We hold patents on several products that need to be manufactured, marketed and delivered.

All are opportunities for someone with the ingenuity to make something happen.

We are designing a data base that will contain each citizen's talents, abilities and desires where another citizen can query the database for the talent and resources needed for a project. They will also be able to take advantage of the labor pool and realize their dream of being their own boss.

Others find comfort in knowing that here in Agape' is an atmosphere where free thinking, endless dreaming and imagination are rewarded. We encourage our citizens to be creative. To share their ideas and inventions with the community inventor through our methods of secure communication. All ideas that are used will be paid for and the originator will receive their fair share of any profit derived from the development of that idea. Your idea may be used by more than one individual and more than one of your ideas may be used at the same time. If your idea is for a large project that will generate many other smaller opportunities and businesses, you will receive compensation from each of them according to their ability to generate income.

What would you really like to do with the rest of your life?

Are you in a position to develop yourself and be creative? If so, do you have the resources that you need to achieve your goals? Let us help. Become a citizen of Agape' and see how God intended for His people to live and develop if Adam and Eve had continued to live in the Garden.

We can all get along. We can all realize our dream. We can all become useful citizens and contribute to the destiny of mankind.

This is our chance to correct the mistakes of the past. We will remember the past to know what mistakes were made. We will look at the present to see the consequences of those actions. From these, together we will build a future that will reflect the true brotherhood of man.

Christianity requires faith. To live a Christian life requires action.

TO THE FUTURE[8]

Hi my friends:

Thought I would touch bases with you before the end of the year. Hope you and yours take an ounce of precaution in whatever you do to celebrate. Thanks so very much for being my friend.

I hope we survive into the new millennium without a hassle!!! I thank the Lord for my health, my right mind and a strong belief in Him. I will continue to pursue the goals that I believe were divinely placed on my shoulders. This quest makes me feel alive. I feel that my life will not have been in vain. I have never been so happy (even though I don't have the financing I desperately need) as I am now.

I've been way up, and I have come far, so far down. The journey prepared me to except this task. We made a mistake this year. We (let them) slipped something in on us while we were looking the other way. In the new millennium, we will have a major battle trying to undo it.

I see many challenges for us in the next millennium. I wish we all could take advantage of the opportunity that is knocking at our door.

If you haven't been bitten by the Computer Bug, you ought run out and change that! If you don't understand the implications of the Internet and E-commerce, you need to get back in a learning mode – there's so much we need to know so we can communicate with the next generation.

But, if for some reason you don't or won't heed this message, I promise you that I will continue to carry this fight until you do, or I die. The currency for the new millennium is KNOWLEDGE!!

---

[8] Written December 19, 1999

CHAPTER SEVEN: Poems

BE A PARENT

I see Daddy going one way,

and I ask where,

He says,

I'm going my own way.

I see mommy going another way,

and I ask where.

She says,

I'm going my own way -

Different from Daddy.

SO,

All that is left for me,

since I love them both,

is to find a way of my own -

different from either.

Who's way will be right?

But even now as I think,

Oh how I wish that even if mommy and daddy

chose the wrong way,

I wish they could choose the same way,

so I could just follow their lead.

CONTEMPLATION

Let's go OUT-WAY OUT,

Where Nature is herself,

Where man is MAN and a tree is a TREE,

Where waters run endlessly,

Where there is no need

For a spoken language but all communes

And understand.

Where mountains, forest, lakes and sand

Loom greater than the greatest MAN.

Let us humble ourselves to the Greatness around,

And contemplate from whence we came.

DOORS

In the matters of Our Lord,

Doors are closed, but we may open some of them;

Doors are open also, and we will close many of them.

BUT,

The *Doors* that My Lord opens can only be closed by Him, and

The *Doors* My Lord closes can only be opened by Him.

And in these days,

I see many ***Doors*** opening and closing.

GLIMPSE OF HEAVEN

I got a glimpse of Heaven today
Soon I hope to be on my way
But, until then, I will shout and pray
I heard his voice and came outside
As the thunder and lightning filled
The sky
I raised my arms in joyous praise
In rhythm with the sounds and
I truly was amazed as
The clouds formed His face
Then others moved to reveal
This most beautiful place
I called to my mother
Though she was long gone from here
To come and witness this revelation
She too marveled at the sight
The clouds formed trees and mountains
And flowing streams with rays of light
Then His face and this grand display
Became heavenly clouds again
I was amazed at this sight and
To see my mother, again, in heaven
I will see both again someday
But until then I shall continue to do His will
And shout and pray
"Hallelujah"

HEAVEN

HEAVEN is when all Nations, Planets

And Galaxies become one Brotherhood

of Men.

And Knowledge increases to the point,

Where modern Man can bring to LIFE

All PEOPLE of the Past.

These PEOPLE are now one Brotherhood.

SENILITY

I remember events and things from

The old days – long ago

Like they happened just yesterday

It's the things that happened

Just yesterday

That I have trouble remembering

CHAPTER EIGHT: Anecdotes

These articles are written to create awareness in you and to stimulate a desire for more understanding. If you would like to receive these articles as they are inspired and written, you may provide me with your E-mail address. You may prefer to receive your copy by Fax or regular mail. If so, please include your mailing information.

LIGHTNING

(Why would I want to settle down now?)

One day, in April, while driving back from a bowling league in Southeast Los Angeles, on my way to my next league, I found myself running a little late. I was feeling good about the way my team had performed. I had scored extremely well. I remember that it was an overcast day and the time was very close to 4:00 pm. The traffic in Los Angeles was, bumper to bumper as usual. For those drivers who don't know the secret moves, it moves even slower. I maneuvered to the outside lane, hit the gas and put in a different tape. This lane will usually be clear until I'm ready to change to the Santa Monica freeway. This tape is jamming, Marvin Gaye singing his greatest hits. At this rate I'll just make it to my lanes on time. The traffic lane to my left is bumper to bumper, no one seems to realize how open this lane is! I'm traveling at 50 mile per hour and there's no traffic in front of me. I prepare to make the next move. The music on the tape reminds me of how wonderful things are going in my life. I feel good, exhilarated, and powerful. I know my team will need me to bowl over my average this evening. They know that when I don't bring a lady with me, I do much better. Today will be a good day. I have to speed up to make a smooth lane change, that just right move. The traffic in the intersection is not so kind. People, who don't know how to maneuver, become obstacles in traffic. Those who do, become competitors and others become allies. I proceed to the exit lane headed for the transition ramp.

My 1976 Dodge Maxi-van is big and powerful. It responds as always, just as I expect, and I accelerate through the curve. The power of the engine becomes more and more evident and I can depend on it to get me out of tight spots.

While all this maneuvering was going on, I never noticed that the sky was changing. Clouds had rolled in and it now looked liked it was about to rain. Coming out of the long looping curve I found myself in the fast lane, but I needed to be in the exiting lane which comes up real fast at this intersection. Without warning there was a great burst of light. My first thought was, "Wow! What was that?" Then I heard a loud booming sound. I thought that someone else or I had crashed. Then through the right side window I saw the great streak of lighting that started high above the city, streaked it's way down in one single jagged bolt, curved twice then jumped to the right side window and exploded all around me. At the same time, I jerked both of my hands from the steering wheel and held them high in the air and held my breath for what seemed like an eternity. There was not a sound from the loud music, from the roaring engine, no from the traffic. "Well, was I dead?" I looked around and could see giant leaping sparks all around my van. They seem to surround it with a dance of celebration as though they were welcoming me home.

My van was still in the fast traffic lane. I grabbed the wheel; still no music but the radio light was on. The traffic around me seemed to be moving in slow motion and I couldn't hear sounds from any of the cars. I thought to myself, "Is this what happens when you die? My team will miss me. They need me. I hope they win. Will I be missed? What's happening? I'm still moving. Can I change anything about this time?" Then, I heard a deafening roar. Iit was the sound of many engines. Traffic was again moving at normal speed. Out of sheer instinct I moved from the fast lane over one lane. "Well, I can still steer", I thought, and then I moved over to the exiting lane. I took my foot off the accelerator and just coasted along with the flow of traffic as I exited the freeway.

I looked at the other drivers to see if any one looked as though they had experienced the same thing.

The traffic was back to normal. I could see the same idiots making dumb moves and the impatient jerks cursing them out. The loud roar has faded into background noise of the traffic, but it's still there. What happened? I'm going to be late, but how do I explain this? When I arrived at the exit everything seemed normal. I was not injured - well, not injured physically. There were no signs of an accident, but the music still couldn't be heard. I reached up and turned the tape off. As I made the right turn onto Crenshaw Boulevard, I reached over and rolled down the passenger side window, then rolled down my window. The air was thick and seemed particularly humid. As I wiped the sweat from my forehead, I thought, "Wow, it's good to be alive! I'm probably going to bowl crappy." As I thought about it, I realized that something very special had happened and I would spend many hours trying to understand just what it meant.

This incident, on the way to the bowling alley, would change my whole life. It has caused me to consider (contemplate) what I should do with this future, since I still seem to have one. Trying to explain the events just creates more questions. I realized just how lonesome life could be, especially, if there is no one with whom I can share these things.

My pastor preached a sermon: "One is not a whole number." He gave reasons why man's nature is to become two by finding a mate and raising a family.

GET HERE IF YOU CAN

There once was a man of above-average means but not wealthy or even well off. This man lives a fairly good life, which takes him in three very different directions.

I will call him Ben. Ben was Religious with worldly attributes, but because of his associations he is being considered for membership in the Masons and as an elder (deacon) in his church, which he attends because of one of his girlfriends.

On his new job, Ben begins to meet co-workers. He begins to date casually; he visits all of the local watering holes, but is not really happy with the ladies he meets. One day he meets a lady who seems very friendly. They talk. She is a Jehovah Witness and invites him to a Revival at her church. She stood him up. Later, she brought a series of sermons from the revival and let him listen to a couple of them. He ends up ordering a set of the tapes. He listens to these tapes over and over to the point that they begin shaping his moral outlook and beliefs toward church. His barber always plays tapes of religious music. During a conversation, his barber invites him to her church.

After visiting this church, he was totally turned off, because of the congregation. Back home his church had 800 members; this little congregation was about the size of his old church's choir (50 members). Even though there was no definite place (church) that he liked, he began to realize that he really enjoyed the fellowship of church-going people.

While watching TV one evening, he saw a news program where a black minister was being interviewed. At the end of the interview the newscaster said if you would like to help, you can contact Reverend McKinney at The Mount Zion Baptist Church. Two weeks later, one of the workers at his job expressed a desire to do something. After talking, they decided to go to church. He remembered the name of the church and suggested they go there.

This co-worker was an outside supplier in Seattle on loan and drove a company car, a new Cadillac, which they drove to church. The experience at this church was much more to his liking: Large church, over 2,000 members; five choir; large Sunday school. They both eventually joined this church. Mount Zion Baptist Church became the center of his social life.

The church required new members go through a series of seven classes before they become full members. The classes were run continuously so a new member could start with any class and eventually complete the series.

The Sunday before he joined, a young lady about 33 years old, had joined and started her series of classes one week before him, but they were in the same series of classes (only one class taught each Sunday). This lady, Jaynell and her 16-year-old daughter Renee were in the class. There were 7 new members in this class. Each person had to do a self introduction and tell their background. It was plain to see that the lady was interested in Ben: "My name is Jaynell Higgins. My daughter and I have lived in this area for 8 years. I am recently widowed and am looking for stability in my life. It's very hard raising three young children alone. We have been coming to this church for two months. The warm fellowship and reliance on the Bible leads me to think this is a good place to get the spiritual help and guidance I need. This is my second class and I think they are great."

"My name is Benjamin Smith. I moved to this area about four months ago. I work at Boeing. I have been looking for a church home since I arrived here. The first time I heard Reverend McKinney Speak, the hairs stood up on my head. Then the choir sang and I knew that this was where I belonged. I think these classes are a great way to find out what is happening in the church and where my talents can best be used to serve God."

The other members introduced themselves also but all he was thinking was that he was going to do this every Sunday for the next five weeks. He had to figure out a way to talk to her before the classes ended. Even if he didn't, he thought, they would still have the bond of these classes.

The next Sunday, Renee came up to him and asked if he was married. He replied that he was not and asked why she wanted to know. She said her mom wanted to invite him over for dinner, but she didn't know if he was free. She said "I like you, you and mom would be good together. I know she likes you. So, how about having dinner with us?" He said, "Well, you let me talk this over with your mom, but I think I would like having dinner."

They had dinner and began to date. He found her to be a good woman with strong family values, a very sexy mom, and forward. She was looking for a permanent relationship, marriage. She owns her home and car, has a good job, and was lonely.

Ben likes her and the children. He has heavy financial obligations (taxes) and is trying to get on his feet. She is the first lady he has met at this new social haven. But other ladies are giving him the eye. He is not willing to commit. She finally gives him an ultimatum to declare his intentions. He explains his situation and hopes she will understand. A few weeks later, she calls him. During the conversation she asks him about his friend. His friend asked her out to a movie and she wondered how he would feel if she went. Things were never the same between them. Desert Storm took her to another part of the country before they could resolve things.

Many people grow up around the church. They go for reasons of their own, but really haven't committed their lives to God. Being a Christian is something he believes in but there are so many questions that Ben needs answers to, that he really haven't pushed the issue. Those around him see a person who believes and has joined church and is trying. He is handsome, well dressed and worldly. Most of his past is sketchy and lack detail. He wants to study the word. He has even brought the message a few times. He would like to have prayer in the home but can't seem to get it going.

Through different times and circumstances, he has been in several different church denominations. Now he is in a new state working. Because of the things from his past, he is glad to be in the new environment. He can now set his standards to live by. He chooses to lay down a set of principals (for him) to live by. He will date women of any race but looks for a relation only with a black woman. He believes in looking professional on his job, has good work habits and loves to help his fellow workers.

He meets an older person that takes a liking to him at church. While in the new city he meets a lady and begins dating. They now attend church together. They do not live together but could easily do so, if not for the church. He begins attending Sunday school and is well liked. He sings in the choir.

Through this association, he is asked to join the Masonic Lodge. Also, he is being considered as a candidate for the Trustee Board or Deacon Board. (The fact that he is not married could prevent him from seriously considering the Deacon Board.)

Recalling things from his past, he realizes that he has had some very interesting experiences with "Church" folk. The first time he "DID IT" was in church. The best youth fellowship Ben ever had was at his church. He met Malcolm X when he spoke at his church. He developed interest in singing there and was propositioned by his choir director (a man). From his association with church, choir and friends, he had to decide just where he stood on many sensitive social issues.

He was quickly becoming an influence to the other youth at church and began giving lectures at the local junior high schools on preparing for the future-

How to become a productive member of society:

They must decide what they want out of life.
Find out what is required to achieve it.

Determine if they are willing and able to pay the price: Education, talent, hard work, and persistence.

Where and how do you to proceed toward achieving their goals? It takes just as much effort to be bad as it does to be good. Whichever path you choose, you must be willing to accept the consequences of your decision. Usually, when you decide to take the good path, the consequences will be that you will become a role model for others and be responsible for showing (even teaching) others. This helps foster self esteem and embeds good values, invariably brings you a good financial base to support you and your family.

On the other hand, if you choose to take the bad side of society's life, you must be willing to accept the punishment and scorn of society. If you work hard, you possibly can amass a good fortune, for a while. But in the long run, you lose.

Ben lives a very worldly, loose life. He struggles to survive for a period while things go wrong (tragic) around him. During this time, he resorts to dealing with a criminal element but stays on the fringe of commitment to real criminal behavior. He sold hot merchandise, acted as a go-between (procurer) for those who had and those who wanted, for a percentage. He used drugs socially and had a philosophy about the use of pot versus the use of other drugs. Does not smoke or drink. He advocates the legalizing of pot. His lady is divorced with two children. She is having a rough time financially and had bad luck with past relationship. She would like stability in her life and a future with a good man. She would like to have a good relationship.

Imagine how you would feel if everything you hoped for in life suddenly fell apart.

Ben was a young man going to college. He was a straight "A" student in high school but couldn't get a scholarship because he is black. He was elected student body president and had some great accomplishments: Fuller Brush Man of the Year. His Junior College Government Association decided to name the Walkway on campus after him but the School Board cancelled it the next year. Influential members of the school and community were grooming him for politics. His parents are very proud. Then the announcement came: "Today, in Dallas, Texas, the President of the U.S. was shot and killed by a sniper." Shortly thereafter, "Today, in Selma, Alabama, Dr. Martin Luther King was shot and killed by a sniper."

These events changed his life. He no longer wanted to run for office as a politician and die in office. It took a long time for him just to begin to work on other politician's campaigns. Then, while working on his party's campaign, he sat watching the election and heard: "Someone has shot and killed Bobby Kennedy at the Hilton Hotel." This was too much for him. He lost faith in humanity. Then the demons began to come out.

Ben is a well-educated man, from formal education to street savvy. He has definite values about the way people should live and how the government should function. He was being groomed for politics until certain tragedies occurred and he lost hope and his desire to serve. Yet he feels the need to participate. Even joined a union and may run for president of the union. His life brought him in contact with a beautiful lady with political hopes. She cares for him and respects his views. She has been passed over twice for political considerations and now is becoming disillusioned. A good marriage would relief all of the pressures and frustrations she is feeling and they have a good relationship.

These three different lifestyles seem to ebb in and out of his life while he is having various degrees of success and periods of peril or danger. He never reaches notoriety to the point that any part of his past or present life becomes a hindrance to whatever he decides to do with his life.

His doctor calls and gives him bad news. Through a series of events he is forced to consider his future in light of one woman (marriage) to settle that. He thinks the world of all three ladies. Even though the three ladies were not always in his life, they became close enough that love still exists and could become a beautiful future for either one of them, with the right commitment from Him.

It is hard for him to choose, so he comes up with this brilliant idea to send a message to each one and see which lady understands it and will know who it is from, and realize that he is finally proposing. This message is a tape with specific songs out of their relationship. Songs that mean everything to him as far as his willingness to devote himself to her – love her forever and settle down, a lasting marriage.

The tape ends with the song "Get Here If You Can." Then he waits to see if either one comes, calls or communicates in anyway.

The story ends as he comes home and the phone rings.

You decide: Guess which one called?

One of the ladies calls on the phone and response positively to his proposal. Which lady? They could get together and live happily ever after.

All three ladies call, then he really has to search himself and decide what he really wants to do.

RAIN ON ME

Today I drove to Portland. On the way back something strange happened.

I was listening to my favorite tape and cruising at 74 miles per hour. The time was about midnight. The sky could barely be seen but I could see that there were no clouds that suggested rain. It had been raining on the drive down.

Suddenly, it started to rain. Slowly, then building gradually to a strong rain. I turned on the wipers to intermittent first. The rain forced me to change that to high, then to continuous. About 10 seconds after the wipers were on continuous; the rain came to a quick stop. I then turned the wipers off. The rain again started, got heavier and heavier causing me to use my wipers. This repeated about six or seven times before I began to pay attention to what was happening.

I began to experiment with what I thought was a strange occurrence. I waited for the rain to slow and instead of turning them off, I turned my wipers to the lowest intermittent level possible. The rain did not start again. I noticed the number of other vehicles close to me. I seem to be in a very large comfort zone. Traffic was a ways ahead and behind me. I like to have some distance between the traffic ahead and behind so I can relax a little. If something happens, I have plenty time to react.

I turned the wipers completely off. I looked to see if there were signs of rain.

The sky seemed to be a uniform gray. Within a minute, the pattern of rain started again. Slow at first, then increasing to a hard rain. I turned the wipers to high and within 10 seconds the rain slowed then stopped. I spent long time thinking about what happened. This is what I concluded.

What I think is, the rain was falling only around my car. The conditions of my music at the high volume, the particular selections, the speed that I was driving caused the car to vibrate just so, the conditions of the area from Portland to Olympia (the Capital) all combined to cause the condition that produced rain where I drove. In retrospect, I remember when being struck by lightning couldn't get my attention. Now I listen to the falling rain.

THE RIGHT THING

Recently, my job required me to move to another location. When I moved into my new area, I found that the person who used to sit there had left things in one of the desk drawers and trash in two wastebaskets.

My first thought was to get upset and move the wastebaskets over to where the person is now located. He left a bunch of change in the center desk drawer and other personnel items. I was tempted not to tell him and keep the change. He has been nice to me since the first day I moved over to this department. He has not arrived at work yet, so I don't know how I am going to react.

I emptied the shopping bag that I used to bring in my things. I put my things in the other drawers and on the top of my desk. I arranged my computer and the telephone and the in baskets. I chose a permanent spot for my attaché case and decided where to put those trash baskets.

A few minutes later, he arrived and spoke to me. He asked if everything was alright. I mentioned that there were things in the desk and he apologized and removed them right away.

When I rearranged the peripheries of my Catia terminal, I noticed that the table it sets on is about half an inch lower than my desk. The mouse plate is located so it sets on the table and butts up against my desk. When I move the mouse, it hits the edge of the desk and causes me to lift it up to be able to select data located at the bottom of the Catia screen. That became annoying to me and caused me to look for a solution. After close examination, I figured that I could raise the mouse plate a little and the mouse would slide onto my desk and solve my problem. Perhaps a magazine would work, if I just had a magazine of the right thickness.

My new area was clean and empty except for the drawer in the desk and the two wastebaskets. When I was temporarily located in my boss's office, I accumulated several plots (print-outs). Some had served their usefulness and were ready to be discarded. Since I didn't want to leave anything in his office, not even in his wastebasket, I folded the plots and brought them with me. I could throw them away later. Two of these plots lay on my desk and seemed like the right thickness. I tried putting them under the mouse plate. They almost fit perfectly. The interference now is barely noticeable, but is still there. The plots are larger than the mouse plate, so it really didn't look good. In time, this could become an eye sore. I really like things neatly arranged. I need to find a better solution, but this would work for now.

I decided to empty the wastebaskets. In one of them was a stack of papers stapled together. They were in a larger stack of papers that were standing on edge. I could see that they were not crumpled or soiled. I tried the stack under the mouse plate. The thickness was perfect. I could have removed some of the sheets if needed, but there was no need. The sheets being 8 ½ x 11 in size fit perfectly under the mouse plate. My area is nice and neat!

Moral of this story:

Hold true to yourself. If you can pass the test God will give you the reward and supply all your needs.

LOVE AND MARRIAGE

Wouldn't it be wonderful if everyone that got married was perfectly matched?

Remember this: I have made many mistakes in my life and will make others. People are human, so they make mistakes.

If you think you have found the perfect person, your marriage is doomed to failure.

If you believe you have found the perfect mate for you, that's love.

Our imperfections will cause us to make mistakes, but our love and belief in why we got married should keep us together in spite of the mistakes we surely will make.

The most important thing is that we know that the vows we take will not change the imperfections in us, but that no matter what, the vows will be honored and we will stay together and love each other forever.

FOREVER is just that - forever. Anything else is just a contract.

THE AMERICAN DREAM

Well, here I am in this big city, living The American Dream. I'm fifty-four years old, fairly good looking, especially for my age, driving a late model luxury car and have very nice apartments in three other metropolitan cities in North America.

A typical day for me begins approximately 6:00 am with a cup of my favorite Blackberry Tea and my day-timer, followed by an hour of phone calls to the states in other time zones. I especially have to communicate with people in Seattle, Las Vegas, Texas and Mississippi. Georgia is coming along well now and I may need to check there also.

Next, I will pamper myself and prepare to challenge the world! I have several appointments for this morning and plans for a long lunch with an old friend whom I haven't seen in six months. Won't he be surprised? Lunch will be at the most popular restaurant in town. Of course, I will pick up the tab. This will start him thinking. His curiosity will inevitably lead to that question: "What are you into these days? Still working at the same place?" It really makes me feel good to know that what I'm about to say will really benefit him.

After lunch I will prepare my notes and review my schedule for the rest of the day. Since I plan on going out tonight, I must remember to have the car washed and waxed. Yesterday, I bought eight new CDs I've been meaning to get ever since I moved here three months ago.

This afternoon, I plan to go to a couple of clubs that are known for the quality of their Happy Hour. Both places cater to people of above-average means that seem to say: "Yes, I earn a comfortable income and can live above the necessities (food, clothing, shelter and transportation)". Places like these are where I really like doing what I do.

Usually, when I go to an establishment like these, I find they are really crowded with some of the most beautiful people I've ever seen. The men show me what competition I have. The young ones flash their signs of success, showing confidence in their achievements. I see $800 suits on wells sculptured physiques, modest but expensive accessories. Well-polished $500 shoes and little leather business card holders... networking, you know.

The ladies, on the other hand, really bring out the best in me. While driving to the club, I know I will be spotted three or four times. Heads certainly will turn. The ladies will be appropriately attired, (sexy but business), exhibiting restrained exuberance, with their eyes on the prize. Some lucky guy will answer most of the questions right and that's All She Wrote! Now me, some lucky lady will ask that inevitable question, "So what do you do?" Now the fun begins. "Well, I own my own business. It covers six states and allows me to travel a lot. It requires me to have homes in several states. I enjoy working for myself". When she asks, "Well what do you actually do?" I will tell her, "I make money. Last year I made three of my employees quite wealthy." I get great pleasure out of that.

It excites me to see how they react. The attention is great! I usually have my choice of the real prizes of the evening. The best part is that I know I am really the lucky one. I get to socialize, wine and dine the most attractive women and spend my money generously every night. The people of my choosing will be rewarded beyond their wildest dreams. I will show them how to live the American Dream. "To own your own business, achieve financial security, and do all the things you always wanted to do".

I have room in my business for a few good people. How about you? Want to work with mean?

Only Dreamers need apply

My Lucky Number

Once upon a time a man wanted something lucky to happen in his meager existence. So he decided to pray for a lucky number. He would play the lotto and solve all his problems.

He owed the back rent and the utilities from where he lived before he got evicted. Since then, things just seem to gradually get worse. Now his phone had been turned off. That meant no phone, no messages and no Internet for his computer.

His faith taught him to believe that the Lord would not put more on you than you can handle. Since things are bad but not unbearable, he thinks that a little break will lead to a complete turnaround. So, he keeps his eyes and ears open for anything that will give him that lucky number.

That afternoon he went to the barbershop for a haircut. As he sat there in the chair looking around, when he could, the wallpaper pattern caught his attention. There was a really nice pattern in the paper that looked like a ribbon of diamonds. The pattern extends from the ceiling to the floor. The wall divided the shop into two areas. One area for basic cuts and the other for more complicated styles.

He counted the patterns and came up with eighteen. He thought, maybe this was a clue to the lucky number he is looking for? But he needed more than two digits in the number, if it is to be the one.

Closer look at the wall showed that all of the strips were not full width. The first edge was just a small part of the pattern. It was barley large enough to see the pattern. The other edge showed a partial pattern also. This one was much larger, about half the width of a full pattern.

He decides that this might work. Instead of eighteen, he really had seventeen and a half. Stated another way - 1750. This is a four-digit number that he could use to place a bet.

The next day, he went to his favorite place and bought a lottery ticket. He played 1-5-7-10-15-17 and 1750 for the daily game.

Guess what numbers won?   1-2-5-7-15-17 for $6 million and the daily game was 1-7-5 for $1 million. If he had trusted his senses and interpreted what he saw correctly, he would be $7 million richer. Could you have done better?

The Art of Dating (for the single man)

Since I've been asked, I will give up some of these pointers to those men who keep asking me to teach a class or write a book.

Consider for a moment that you are newly divorced or separated after eight years of marriage. Now you need to put the pain and disappointment behind you and go on with the rest of your life.

I have a friend that is in this exact situation. He confided in me and after my council, he is feeling better about himself. But when he is at home alone he still gets depressed. One thing for sure, anyone that finds themselves in this situation does not need to stay home. The way to get over this depression is to force yourself to go where there are other people. This is the point I wish to address here.

Where can or should one go. Normally I would not recommend a shopping spree. As long as you don't do major shopping, it's ok. The important thing is to have the right mind set; understand what to do and why. Then do it with this in mind.

I believe one should concentrate on the things in their normal activities. I recommend you stay within your normal routine. You will feel more relaxed.

There will be fewer uncertainties. For those who need to develop a routine, I offer this as a possible example.

I live in Renton, Washington, and shop at the local Fred Meyer shopping center on Rainier Avenue. Shopping at Freddie's gives me opportunities to meet people and not feel out of place. I feel no pressure to socialize, but there are oh so many opportunities.

Remember, you can go to market and look. You don't need to buy anything. This can be fun for singles if you are aware of whom and why people are there. I go to Freddie's enough that I have covered most of the different time periods. I know what to look for.

While you are browsing, check out the women. You can find out a lot about them by observing their shopping carts or baskets. Single women shop for one or two. They seldom buy economy sizes. They buy the special loaf of bread. Many of the things they buy shout "single'. Women love to be helpful to men who can't find things in the market.

Since we all do grocery shopping, why not let your choice of market afford you an opportunity for socializing. The more you visit that market the more employees you will come to know by name. Conversation comes easy between people who know each other's name.

Find a restaurant where you can have dinner and spend Happy Hour. Whenever you find yourself at home and feeling depressed, go out to eat. You should feel comfortable eating hors devours during Happy Hour, or sitting at the bar having a drink. The more often you do this the more comfortable you will feel.

Fred Meyers shares its parking lot with a Mexican restaurant and a video rental store. The video store is filled with people browsing. Check them out. You should develop a routine that is natural for you. Do things you like and need to do. Then become aware of the rules of the engagement. By doing this you will be around lots of interesting people. Be yourself because many of them are checking you out also. So you feel uncomfortable starting a conversation.

Maybe your game is lame. Perhaps you are self conscience. If you stay in your normal comfort zone, go where you normally go, you'll find it easy to be yourself. These days, a man with a good job, who is single and straight, will find that women will be attracted to them.

Your routine may be very simple. You may need to take a look at the things you do. Your routine may be too complicated. If so, don't try to become an expert with all the places you go. Remember this is your life. You will be doing this until your status changes.

Meanwhile, don't panic. Get to know yourself. Learn to like the real you. Work on changing what needs changing.

When strangers meet they usually accept each other as they see them. There's no need for a façade. You will meet many people, male and female, who will like you just as you are.

Sand on the Beach

What do you see when you stand on the beach and look at the sand?

The pessimist might see grit or dirt, something that will cause discomfort if you get it on you or in your shoes.

The pragmatist might see a pretty white blanket, a clean surface to play or stretch out.

The visionary might see a crystal glass, an automobile windshield or a chandelier

If things were the way they should be, you would be the wealthiest person on earth. The concept of manna from heaven teaches us that we should not hoard. There are enough resources in the world to feed and cloth every human being. We could build enough housing for all and provide meaningful uses for everyone's unique talents. Each one and has as much as he or she needs, they would have everything

The New Revelation – Putting It All Together

Character

Character: (Look up definition of Character.)

Describe your character.

Include: reliability, dependability, morals, pride, and personality

What one trait of your character do you like most?

What one trait would you change?

If you were describing yourself over the telephone, to someone you never met, what would you say?

Plan for the future

What do you want to do or be when you grow up?

What do you have to do to achieve that?

How do you plan to live (support yourself)?

How much income will you need?

What type of work will give you that income?

How long do you have to prepare for your future?

When should you prepare?

How can you tell if you are on track?

Are your plans realistic (within your reach)?

Where would you go for help?

At what age do you plan to be able to support yourself?

The Lord Answers

The Lord answers all of my needs. Not sometime in the future, but it seems, as soon as I can formulate them. Yesterday, as Dennis and I walked into Eagles, I noticed a lady walking just ahead and to the side of us. This lady, I could tell, was not a spring chicken, but she looked awfully good to me.

She looked my way and I took the opportunity to speak with a nod. I noticed her smile. I felt good about this possible encounter. I remarked to Dennis that I wonder if that fellow just ahead of her was with her. He said, "You aren't

86

going to let that stop you, are you?" Yes it would but I wasn't about to give up until I knew for sure.

As she entered the store, we were just behind her with the man a step or two ahead of her. I watched as she glanced over her shoulder and slowed up. The man kept going. She turned and stopped at the courtesy counter. That was my chance to say something.

"Is that fellow with you?"

"He's my son," was her answer. Now it was up to me to (flirt) see if she was interested in my attention.

"I just wondered because I like what I see", I said. "Are you married?

"No, are you?" she replied.

"No. My name is Willie Harvey. What's yours?"

"Just listen to you. You're a big flirt," she said with a twinkle in her eye.

"Yes, I admit it. How could I not be around you?" I asked. "What shall I call you? May I call you?"

"You're not married," she asked again, accepting my nod as an answer. "What do you do? Are you a construction worker?"

"No, I own my own business. I am contract engineer and I am trying to get back into Boeing."

"What kind of business do you have?" she asked with interest.

"Har-V Promotions, Inc., but I don't have time to explain it now," I told her.

"What do you do?" she asked.

"My corporation's creed is 'To serve mankind,' I explained briefly. "May I call you? What gorgeous eyes you have. I could get in them." She smiled and I knew I had a chance. I could tell she was enjoying this encounter.

"You can call me at my office," she said.

"What do you do?" I asked.

"I run a newspaper. I have a card somewhere," she said as she opened her purse. I was very surprised.

"You're joking, aren't you?" I asked.

"No I really do. I know I have a card in here," as she searched through her purse. Other words were exchanged.

I told her, "I would like to kiss each of those freckles."She blushed and smiled. I could see her wondering as the possibilities passed through her mind.

"What's your name?" I asked her, looking into her eyes.

"Elizabeth," she answered, "and here is my card."

"I know this paper. You work for The Fact?" I exclaimed.

"No, I own it," was her reply.

"Why did you ask if I were a construction worker?" I said, changing the subject.

"My friend is remodeling a bathroom for a friend," she explained. "That's why we are here. I'm sure glad we came when we did." As it turned out, she needed someone to finish some remodeling that had been started but never finished. I mentioned that Dennis probably could do it or find someone to finish it. I introduced them.

"I'm really glad we met and I look forward to seeing you," I said as we parted.

Just the other day I was thinking to myself (talking with the Master), how much I needed someone to help me do things with Har-V Promotions, Inc. One thing I really need is publicity. She could be the answer to my prayer.

I realize that if we do spent any time together, I will get a chance to tell her about my corporation and the Philosophy. I will be able to explain what I'm trying to do and show her my revelation for mankind. In time she could become a willing participant in this quest.

I am prepared to make this worth her while. I think she will like what she finds out and will be willing to help. The way she could help is to write about Har-V Promotions.

Har-V Promotions, Inc. needs someone to head up the Publicity Department. I think she would be a perfect fit.

As time goes on, she would have exclusive rights to all the breaking news from Har-V Promotions, Inc. Her paper is dependent upon advertising to remain solvent. Har-V Promotions, Inc. would be her biggest sponsor. In time, *The Facts Newspaper* could become the official source of publicity for my Corporation. I know I'm going to enjoy getting to know Elizabeth. I know she will enjoy the things we do and our conversations. This will be enough, but what possibilities!

Thank you Lord for all that you do through me.

BUILT ON LOVE, TRUST AND RESPECT

There once was a man and woman who were dating. The woman wanted a committed relationship; so the man came up with a little test. He bought an engagement ring and put it in a banana split. He carefully wrapped it and went to see her. After much thought, he said, I've come to the conclusion that

I might not be exactly what you are looking for but I offer you all that I have.

After thinking it over, she responded "ok I'll take it, what are you offering"? He opened up the beautifully prepared bonanza split. Her disappointment couldn't be hidden. This is what you are offering me? And you know I don't like strawberry ice cream! She left it and walked away.

I knew you weren't listening to me, the man answered. She didn't understand the significance of the banana split and asked him to explain.

What would you have done?

(Think about it before you read further)

The man explained:

If you had accepted what I offered you, you would have everything you could get from me. The split represents me. Some things I do you will not care for but you must take the bad with the good. If you had eaten the parts you like you would have found the surprise hidden inside.

What would you have done?

(Think about it before you read further)

Finally catching on, she took the split and poked around in it with a fork until she found the surprise (ring). She kissed him and shouted YES! Then she ran off to show her friends.

If this were you what would you do?

If you were the lady;

If you were the man;

Make sure you are ready to except what you ask for.

Asking is a two way street.

If you love me, accept my faults.

Love opens one up to hurt. You must trust each other.

Respect will make you listen when the one you love speaks.

PEARLS OF WISDOM

Over the years I've had many thoughts on matters of great diversity, which you may find interesting, humorous, or informative. Most of all, I hope they cause you to open up your mind and consider the deeper meanings.

NO LEGACY, NO WORTH
BELIEFS ARE SEASONAL
IS THE CUP HALF -EMPTY OR HALF- FULL?
DAY ONE - ONE DAY
TO STAND STILL IS TO SEE THE END.
I CAME INTO THE WORLD ALONE
    BUT NEVER AGAIN WILL I BE.
MY FAMILY IS ALL OF MANKIND.
INTELLIGENCE REQUIRES (COMES AT) BIRTH.
    EDUCATION REQUIRES STUDY.
        WISDOM REQUIRES EXPERIENCE.
CARRY THE BOOK IN YOUR HAND.
    BUT,
    CARRY THE KNOWLEDGE IN YOUR HEAD.
ONE KNOWS THE LENGTH OF HIS JOURNEY
    BY WHERE HE DECIDES TO STOP.
EVERY DAY I WAKE UP TO A NEW WORLD.
EVERY NIGHT I GO TO SLEEP KNOWING
    I HAVE PREPARED THE WAY
    FOR TOMORROWS NEW WORLD
CLOSE YOUR EYES - NOT YOUR MIND.
IF THE MOON IS MADE OF GREEN CHEESE?
    THEN ALL THE SKY IS A BOWL OF SOUP
    AND ALL THE STARS ARE CRACKERS

IT'S BETTER TO BE GOOD

THAN TO BE THOUGHT OF AS GOOD.

GOOD AND EVIL REQUIRE EACH OTHER.

FIENDSHIP

If you wish to be my friend,

You should first understand

My meaning of friendship

And the obligations and

Responsibilities that (it) implies

It takes two, each doing their part....

Being there in time of need, and....

Having needs to be there for!

CREDITS

People tell me things. People make references and statements in speeches, sermons and entertainment media. These things lead me in my formulation of much of what you read here. They are too numerous to list here and honestly, I don't remember all of them.

To all of them I give credit and any of them that need special acknowledgment, I will be happy to oblige.

Any quotes or direct reference is listed here or on the appropriate page.

Thanks to Almighty God for the insight to use me and to place at my disposal the collective wisdom and thinking of the following individuals: (List names)

Pat Henry	Barbra Lott	Gerald L. Smith
Evone Riley	Sharon Pickett	Louise Braxton
Cynthia Charleston	Dennis Corbett	Lawrence Fox
Joan Catlett	Crystal M. Whitney	Maurice DeeDee McGhee
Rev Samuel B. McKinney	Mrs. Louise McKinney	Dr. Martin L. King

Mohandas Karamchand Gandhi was born on October 2, 1869, in Porbandar, near Bombay. His family belonged to the Hindu merchant caste Vaisya. His father had been prime minister of several small native states. Gandhi was married when he was only thirteen years old.

When he was nineteen he defied custom by going abroad to study. He studied law at University College in London. Fellow students snubbed him because he was an Indian. In his lonely hours he studied philosophy. In his reading he discovered the principle of nonviolence as enunciated in Henry David Thoreau's "Civil Disobedience," and he was persuaded by John Ruskin's plea to give up industrialism for farm life and traditional handicrafts--ideals similar to many Hindu religious ideas. (Ruskin: Thoreau.)

From Compton's Interactive Encyclopedia Deluxe © 1998, The Learning Company, Inc.

Page Left Blank Intentionally.